BARRON

JOSEPH
CONRAD'S

Heart of Darkness & The Secret Sharer

BY

Jeremy Jericho

SERIES EDITOR

Michael Spring
Editor, *Literary Cavalcade*
Scholastic Inc.

BARRON'S EDUCATIONAL SERIES, INC.

ACKNOWLEDGMENTS

We would like to acknowledge the many painstaking hours of work Holly Hughes and Thomas F. Hirsch have devoted to making the *Book Notes* series a success.

All inquiries should be addressed to:
Barron's Educational Series, Inc.
250 Wireless Boulevard
Hauppauge, New York 11788

Library of Congress Catalog Card No. 84-18530

International Standard Book No. 0-8120-3418-X

Library of Congress Cataloging in Publication Data
Jericho, Jeremy.
    Joseph Conrad's Heart of darkness & The secret sharer.

    (Barron's book notes)
    Bibliography: p. 134
    Summary: A guide to reading "Heart of Darkness" and
"The Secret Sharer" with a critical and appreciative mind.
Includes background on the author's life and times, sample
tests, term paper suggestions, and a reading list.
    1. Conrad, Joseph, 1857–1924. Heart of darkness.
2. Conrad, Joseph, 1857–1924. Secret sharer. [1. Conrad,
Joseph, 1857–1924. Heart of darkness. 2. Conrad,
Joseph, 1857–1924. Secret sharer. 3. English literature
—History and criticism] I. Title.
PR6005.04H475   1984   823'.912   84-18530
ISBN 0-8120-3418-X (pbk.)

PRINTED IN THE UNITED STATES OF AMERICA

456   550   9876543

CONTENTS

ADVISORY BOARD

HOW TO USE THIS BOOK

You have to know how to approach literature in order
to get the most out of it. This *Barron's Book Notes* volume follows a plan based on methods used by some
of the best students to read a work of literature.

Begin with the guide's section on the author's life
and times. As you read, try to form a clear picture of
the author's personality, circumstances, and motives
for writing the work. This background usually will
make it easier for you to hear the author's tone of
voice, and follow where the author is heading.

Then go over the rest of the introductory material—such sections as those on the plot, characters,
setting, themes, and style of the work. Underline, or
write down in your notebook, particular things to
watch for, such as contrasts between characters and
repeated literary devices. At this point, you may want
to develop a system of symbols to use in marking your
text as you read. (Of course, you should only mark up
a book you own, not one that belongs to another person or a school.) Perhaps you will want to use a different letter for each character's name, a different
number for each major theme of the book, a different
color for each important symbol or literary device. Be
prepared to mark up the pages of your book as you
read. Put your marks in the margins so you can find
them again easily.

Now comes the moment you've been waiting
for—the time to start reading the work of literature.
You may want to put aside your *Barron's Book Notes*
volume until you've read the work all the way
through. Or you may want to alternate, reading the
Book Notes analysis of each section as soon as you have
finished reading the corresponding part of the origi-

nal. Before you move on, reread crucial passages you don't fully understand. (Don't take this guide's analysis for granted—make up your own mind as to what the work means.)

Once you've finished the whole work of literature, you may want to review it right away, so you can firm up your ideas about what it means. You may want to leaf through the book concentrating on passages you marked in reference to one character or one theme. This is also a good time to reread the *Book Notes* introductory material, which pulls together insights on specific topics.

When it comes time to prepare for a test or to write a paper, you'll already have formed ideas about the work. You'll be able to go back through it, refreshing your memory as to the author's exact words and perspective, so that you can support your opinions with evidence drawn straight from the work. Patterns will emerge, and ideas will fall into place; your essay question or term paper will almost write itself. Give yourself a dry run with one of the sample tests in the guide. These tests present both multiple-choice and essay questions. An accompanying section gives answers to the multiple-choice questions as well as suggestions for writing the essays. If you have to select a term paper topic, you may choose one from the list of suggestions in this book. This guide also provides you with a reading list, to help you when you start research for a term paper, and a selection of provocative comments by critics, to spark your thinking before you write.

THE AUTHOR AND HIS TIMES

Joseph Conrad didn't set out to become one of the great English novelists. He didn't set out to be a novelist at all, but a sailor, and besides, he wasn't English. English was his third language and he didn't begin learning it until after he was 20 years old!

He was born Józef Teodor Konrad Korzeniowski in 1857, in an area of Poland that was part of Russia and is now part of the Soviet Union. The Poles were fighting for independence from Russia, and both parents were fiercely engaged in the struggle. Conrad's father was arrested in 1861 for revolutionary activity, and the family was exiled to the remote Russian city of Vologda. On the journey there, four-year-old Conrad caught pneumonia. He remained a sickly child, and he suffered from ill health for the rest of his life.

Conditions in Vologda were grueling. They were too much for Conrad's mother, and although the family was eventually allowed to move to a milder climate, she died of tuberculosis when Conrad was only seven years old. His father's spirit was broken, and so was his health. The Czarist government finally let him return with Conrad to the Polish city of Cracow, but he died there after a year, when Conrad was eleven.

For the next several years Conrad was raised by his maternal grandmother. A stern but devoted uncle, Tadeusz Bobrowski, saw to his education. Bobrowski had a lot to put up with. Conrad wasn't much of a student. (Surprisingly, he didn't show any particular talent for languages; even his Polish could have stood improvement.) What was worse, at the age of 14 the boy got the unheard-of notion—unheard-of in land-locked Poland, that is—that he wanted to become a sailor. Bobrowski packed him off for Europe with a tutor who was supposed to talk sense into him, but the tutor ended up pronouncing Conrad "hopeless" and giving up the struggle. In 1874, at the age of 16, Conrad traveled to Marseilles to learn the seaman's trade.

During his four years in the French merchant marine, Conrad sailed to the West Indies and possibly along the coast of Venezuela, and he had an adventure smuggling guns into Spain. He participated fully in the cultural life of Marseilles, and a little too fully in the social life. He got himself into a spectacular mess. Deeply in debt, he invited a creditor to tea one evening and shot himself while the man was on his way over. His uncle received an urgent telegram: "Conrad wounded, send money—come." He did, and he was relieved to find young Conrad in good shape (except for his finances)—handsome, robust, well mannered and, above all, an excellent sailor. The author would later claim, rather romantically, that he got a scar on his left breast fighting a duel.

Since the young man couldn't serve on another French ship without becoming a French citizen, which would have entailed the possibility of being drafted, he signed on at the age of 20 to an English steamer. The year was 1878. For the next 16 years he sailed under the flag of Britain, becoming a British subject in 1886. Life in the merchant marine took him to ports in Asia and the South Pacific, where he gathered material for the novels he still—amazingly—didn't know he was going to write. His depressive and irritable disposition didn't make sea life any easier for him. He quarreled with at least three of his captains, and he continued to suffer from periods of poor health and paralyzing depression.

In 1888 Conrad received his first command, as captain of the *Otago*, a small ship sailing out of Bangkok. It was grueling journey: three weeks to Singapore owing to lack of wind, and the whole crew riddled with fever; from there to Melbourne, Australia, where he decided to resign the command and return to England. The maddening calms of the voyage, and his uncomfortable position as a stranger on his first command, provided the inspiration 21 years later for the outlines of "The Secret Sharer."

Back in England, Captain Korzeniowski (as he was still known) wasn't able to find another command, and so through the influence of relatives in Brussels he secured an appointment as captain of a steamship on the Congo River. At the age of 9, he had put his finger on the blank space in the middle of a map of Africa and boasted, "when I grow up I shall go *there*"; at 32, he was fulfilling a lifelong dream. But the dream quickly turned into a nightmare. "Everything is repellent to me here," he wrote from the Congo. "Men and things, but especially men." The "scramble for loot" disgusted him; the maltreatment of the black Africans sickened him; and as if that weren't enough, he suffered from fever and dysentery that left his health broken for the rest of his life. Though his experiences in Africa were to form the basis of his most famous tale, *Heart of Darkness*, he returned to England traumatized. His outlook, already gloomy, became even blacker.

Though Captain Korzeniowski didn't know it, his sea career was drawing to a close. In 1889 he had started a novel based on his experiences in the East. He worked on it in Africa and on his return, and in 1895 it was published as *Almayer's Folly* by Joseph Conrad. (Years of hearing the British garble "Korzeniowski" convinced him to put something they could pronounce on the title page.) It was, like most of his books over the next two decades, a critical but not a popular success. Writing was an agony for Conrad: he was painfully slow at it, though the necessity of getting paid made him work faster than he liked. As a result of hurry, he never felt satisfied with the finished product. (Of the masterful *Heart of Darkness* he wrote at the time, "it is terribly bad in places and falls short of my intention as a whole.") Marriage and the birth of two sons made his financial strain even more desperate. Periods of intense productivity (such as the mere two months in which he completed *Heart of Darkness*) alternated with periods of despair in which nothing got written, as well as with his recurrent bouts of nervous exhaustion and gout. A description Conrad gave of his father could have described himself: "A man of great sensibilities; of exalted and dreamy temperament; with a terrible gift of irony and of gloomy disposition."

Although Conrad's income from writing remained small, his reputation steadily grew. He could count among his friends and admirers such famous names as Ford Madox Ford, Stephen Crane, H. G. Wells, Bertrand Russell, and his idol, Henry James. Financial security eventually came: in 1910 he was awarded a small pension; an American collector began purchasing his manuscripts; and his novel *Chance*, serialized in 1912 and published in book form two years later on both sides of the Atlantic, became his first bestseller.

Conrad died in 1924 at the age of 66. He had attained international renown, but even then he was popularly regarded mainly as a teller of colorful adventures and sea stories. But his experiments in style and technique exerted a major influence on the development of the modern novel. Since his death, the profundity—and darkness—of his vision have become widely recognized.

Heart of Darkness

THE NOVEL

The Plot

On a boat anchored in the Thames River outside London, a sailor by the name of Marlow observes to several friends that this land was once a place of darkness, an uncivilized wilderness. This reflection leads him to remember an incident in his past, when he commanded a steamboat on the Congo River; his story forms the remainder of the novel.

In his tale Marlow is a young man eager to see the unexplored African jungles. An influential aunt in Brussels secures him an appointment as captain of a Congo steamer. But when he reaches the Company's Outer Station in Africa, he's confronted with a spectacle of black slavery and white greed. In a shady grove he discovers a crew of sickly African workers who have crawled away to die. He also meets the Company's very proper chief accountant, who mentions a certain Mr. Kurtz—a remarkable agent who has sent more ivory back from the jungle than the other agents combined. Marlow's interest in Kurtz will grow eventually into an obsession and become the focus of the story.

After a difficult overland trek, Marlow arrives at the Company's Central Station, where he learns that the steamer he was supposed to command has been wrecked. He meets the local manager, an unlikable and unfeeling man, who mentions that Mr. Kurtz is rumored to be ill at his station upriver and that it's essential to get to him as soon as possible.

One night as the others are fighting a blaze in one of the sheds, Marlow talks with one of the agents at the station, a brickmaker, who speaks of Kurtz with admiration but also resentment at the talents that make him such a likely candidate for promotion. Kurtz, he says, is one of those men who have come to Africa not merely for gain but with the noble idea of spreading enlightenment across the backward continent.

Dozing one evening on the deck of his steamer, Marlow overhears a conversation between the manager and his uncle, an explorer. It's obvious that the manager despises Kurtz—partly for his high ideals and partly because, like the brickmaker, he resents Kurtz's abilities.

After three months of repairs, Marlow, the manager, and a crew of three or four whites and some 30 Africans begin the tedious voyage upriver to Kurtz's station, through a jungle that strikes Marlow as weird, foreboding, and gigantic. Fifty miles below the station they come upon a reed hut with wood stacked for the steamboat and a message for them to approach cautiously.

A couple of mornings later they awaken surrounded by a thick fog through which they hear a tumult of threatening cries. Once the fog lifts they set sail again. Suddenly they're assailed by a shower of arrows. As the white men on board fire hysterically (and ineptly) into the brush, Marlow steers close to the shore to avoid a snag, and his African helmsman gets a spear between the ribs. Marlow jerks at the steam whistle, and as it screeches the attackers flee in terror at the noise. He casts the dead helmsman overboard in order to keep the hungry cannibal crew from being tempted by such a meal.

Soon they arrive at the Inner Station, where they're greeted enthusiastically by a young Russian sailor who has been nursing Kurtz through a grave illness; it was he who left the pile of wood and the message. The wilderness, we learn, preyed on Kurtz's nerves, and he began to go mad; he participated in "unspeakable rites" and scrawled at the end of a high-toned, idealistic report about improving the savages through benevolence, "Exterminate all the brutes!" Although the Russian is a fanatical admirer of Kurtz's brilliance, he admits that Kurtz seized his ivory from the Africans through violence, brutality, and intimidation. Even as he's chattering, Marlow notices that the posts in front of the station house are crowned with heads.

Mr. Kurtz finally appears, borne on a stretcher. Marlow, well aware that Kurtz doesn't really want to leave the jungle where he's treated as a god, knows that with a word to his African army Kurtz could have them all slaughtered. But Kurtz allows himself to be carried aboard the steamer, although a magnificent and ferocious African woman seems ready to lead another attack.

The manager tells Marlow he disapproves of Kurtz—not because of his brutality, but only because his methods have made further plundering of the district temporarily difficult. The young Russian visits Marlow and discloses that the earlier attack on the steamer was ordered by Kurtz; then he steals away into the jungle. He fears the manager who hates the Russian because his ivory trading gives the Company competiton.

Late that night Kurtz escapes and crawls ashore, but Marlow discovers his absence and cuts him off before he reaches his followers' camp. They make a tense departure the next day, surrounded by warriors who seem ready to attack under the leadership of the barbaric woman. But Marlow sounds the whistle and frightens them off.

As they steam back downriver, Kurtz's life slowly ebbs away. On his deathbed he has what seems to be a moment of illumination, of complete knowledge, and he cries out, "The horror! The horror!" before he dies.

Then Marlow too is taken by the fever and very nearly dies. But he survives and returns to Brussels, where, more than a year after Kurtz's death, he pays a visit to Kurtz's Intended, the woman he was engaged to marry. She's still in mourning, heartbreakingly devoted to the memory of a man she thinks was noble and generous to the end. When she pleads that Marlow repeat Kurtz's last words to her, he can't bear to shatter her illusions: "The last word he pronounced was—your name," he lies. She cries out and collapses in tears.

The Characters

Charlie Marlow

Through the first two thirds of *Heart of Darkness*, our curiosity about Kurtz is raised to such a pitch that we may realize only afterward, in thinking about the novel, that the main character isn't Kurtz at all, but Marlow. We find out less about Kurtz than about his effect on Marlow's life. *Heart of Darkness* tells the story of Marlow's spiritual journey—a voyage of discovery and self-discovery.

It seems safe to assume that Marlow is Conrad's stand-in. Marlow was born in England, not Poland, and he never gave up sailing to write; but otherwise the differences between the two men aren't striking. And we know that *Heart of Darkness*, especially in its first half, is heavily autobiographical.

Marlow tends to keep his own counsel: he's always observing and judging, but his politeness covers up the harshness of his judgments and encourages others to speak their minds. The brickmaker and the manager both speak frankly to him because his mask of courtesy hides his contempt for them. (Later, when his experiences have so upset him that he's on the verge of a breakdown, Marlow does speak sarcastically to the manager, and he's never forgiven for it.)

We don't learn much about Marlow's life before the Congo voyage, beyond the simple fact that he is an experienced sailor who has seen the world. But we do get to know Marlow quite well. He is a man of modesty and courage. We know about his modesty from his embarrassment at his aunt's high praises. And we see many examples of his courage, most notably during the attack on the steamer and at Kurtz's escape. At such times Marlow always keeps a cool head; but in telling the story he never emphasizes his own daring or heroism.

Marlow is obviously an excellent sailor, devoted to his work; he enjoys remembering, and making us attentive to, the technical details and difficulties of getting an old steamboat up a shallow river. His fondness for work is at the very base of his system of values. Although you may not like work—nobody does, he admits—it's what keeps you sane, just as it keeps Marlow sane in the jungle. It provides a structure for your life, and if you concentrate on the details of your duties, you won't be tempted by the call of madness, the "darkness" of the unknown that surrounds us.

Marlow is the moral grounding point of the novel, the only white man in the Congo who recognizes the evils of colonialism in Africa. The spectacle of death and enslavement there is overwhelming, so Marlow's responses (as he would probably argue) aren't extraordinarily moral, just normal, the only normal ones we see amid the demented greed of the traders. But Marlow is also the everyman of the novel, the basically decent and intelligent character who stands for all of us. The ugly truths he confronts are truths we all have to face. Marlow learns that he has to acknowledge his own heart of darkness, the call of the primitive in his own nature. (Conrad puts this symbolically when, late in the story, Marlow confuses the pounding of the savage drum with the beating of his own heart.) And this is the lesson he tries to impart to his listeners—and to us.

Kurtz

Almost from the moment Marlow arrives at the Outer Station he starts hearing about Mr. Kurtz— from the accountant, the manager, the brickmaker, and finally from the Russian. And he tells us a lot about Kurtz himself, especially during the long digression that comes just after the attack, a few pages before the end of Chapter II. But Kurtz himself is on the scene for only a few pages, and we learn less about him from observation than we do from what these other characters say about him. In fact, after all the build-up, his appearance may even seem a little disappointing: he never turns out to be as exciting as the "unspeakable rites" we're told he participated in. But Kurtz is more important for what he represents than for what he does—we don't get to see him do much of anything. Although he isn't the subject of the novel (Marlow's spiritual journey is), you could call him the focus, the catalyst to whom the other characters react. He's more present in his effect on others than in himself. Some characters, such as the Russian and the Intended, are defined almost solely by their relationship to him.

But though he isn't strongly present as a personality, as a symbol he's a figure rich with meaning. Kurtz is a microcosm—a whole in miniature—of the white man's failure in Africa: he goes equipped with the finest technology and the highest philanthropic ideals and ends up injuring (even killing) the Africans and stealing their ivory. He reduces technology to the guns he uses to plunder ivory.

Kurtz also shows us the consequence of inadequate self-knowledge. He journeys to Africa eager to do good, and completely unaware of the dark side of his nature, the side that will respond to the call of the primitive. (It's Marlow who comes to know this side of himself.) Kurtz points up one of the morals of Marlow's tale: if you aren't aware of the darkness within you, you won't know how to fight it if you ever need to.

If Marlow stands for work, Kurtz represents the opposite value, talk. Before meeting him, Marlow can imagine him only talking, not doing; and when Marlow does finally come face-to-face with him, Kurtz is so thin from disease that he seems to be little more than a strong, deep voice. His influence on people (the Russian, the Intended, even the accountant and the brickmaker) comes through his eloquent words. He is, fittingly, a journalist (a profession for which Conrad seems to hold little regard: Marlow is disgusted by the "rot let loose in print" in the Belgian papers). One of his colleagues thinks he would have made a fine radical politician: after all, if he could sway individuals by his words, couldn't he sway masses as well? Conrad was conservative in his own politics; he would have disapproved of Kurtz the demagogue, the radical orator.

Actions, Marlow seems to be saying, can't lie; but words can and do. And Kurtz is associated with lies. After explaining that Kurtz (*kurz*) is German for short, Marlow tells us: "Well, the name was as true as everything else in his life—and death. He looked at least seven feet long" (Chapter III). Kurtz's ideals turn out to be lies when he drops them to become a devil-god in the jungle. In fact, there is something contaminating in the aura of lies that surrounds him. Thus, as Marlow is drawn to him, he finds himself almost irresistibly lying (to the brickmaker), and he continues lying even after Kurtz's death (to the Intended).

But Kurtz has one quality that even in his degradation places him on a level above most of the other whites Marlow encounters in Africa. That quality is consciousness. Kurtz recognizes the evil of his actions; in fact, as the Russian informs us, he suffers from that knowledge. The other whites in Africa commit acts (the enslavement and massacre of huge numbers of people) that they don't even recognize as wrong. So when Marlow talks about the "choice of nightmares" represented by the manager and Kurtz, he puts his loyalty with Kurtz, who at least isn't petty, though he is brutal. The manager, on the other hand, is a talentless nobody who in his pettiness still brings suffering to others. The depths to which Kurtz sinks is a measure of the heights he could have risen to.

The Russian

When Marlow finally arrives at Kurtz's Inner Station, he encounters a young Russian sailor whose outfit is so colorfully patched that he reminds Marlow of a harlequin, the traditional Italian clown who dresses in motley. And he's as simple-minded and almost as ridiculous as a clown—a startling instance of innocence in the midst of depravity, and a peculiar contrast to Kurtz. (He also serves as a plot device, filling us in on details about Kurtz we need to know.) Though he is "Kurtz's last disciple" and apparently even witnessed the "unspeakable rites" Kurtz participated in, he's too childlike to have taken part himself. Marlow even admires his adventurous spirit, though he disapproves of his devotion to Kurtz.

But even his devotion makes him sympathetic. He nursed Kurtz through two serious illnesses without medical supplies, and he received little gratitude in return. (Kurtz even threatened to shoot him to get his small hoard of ivory.) In addition to loyalty, his character is marked by "the glamour of youth" and "the absolutely pure, uncalculating, unpractical spirit of adventure." He has wandered the jungles for two years, mostly alone; and he makes his exit headed for more lonely wanderings. He is full of self-doubt; he has no great thoughts and no abilities, he tells Marlow. No wonder such an impressionable youth is mesmerized by "Kurtz's magnificent eloquence."

But the Russian sailor is also a fool. Marlow tells us that a fool is safe from madness in the jungle: you can be "too dull even to know you are being assaulted by the powers of darkness" (Chapter II). The Russian is so awed by Kurtz's ideas ("That man has enlarged my mind," he exclaims) that he becomes morally blind to the evil Kurtz does. Yet he is not malicious himself; in fact, he's one of the very few whites along the Congo who isn't a scoundrel. So it's appropriate that he doesn't work for the odious Company. (His free-agent status, in fact, is what makes the manager want to hang him.)

The Manager

If *Heart of Darkness* has a villain, it's the manager of the Company's Central Station, who accompanies Marlow on the steamboat to the Inner Station. But he's a villain in a rather general sense, standing in Marlow's eyes for all the bloodless bureaucrats who calmly oversee the Company's mass enslavement of the Africans. He has no moral sensibility, just a business sensibility: Kurtz's foulest crimes are, to his mind, "deplorable" only because "the trade will suffer" on account of them (Chapter III).

The manager is a talentless nobody with no special abilities. His Central Station is a chaotic mess. The only claim he has to his position is his hardy constitution: he doesn't catch the tropical diseases that overwhelm other whites (including Kurtz and Marlow). That gives him staying power.

Practically the first thing Marlow says about the manager is, "He was commonplace in complexion, in feature, in manners, and in voice" (Chapter I); and the long description that follows emphasizes his commonness. In this he is certainly the opposite of his rival, Kurtz, of whom Marlow remarks, "Whatever he was, he was not common" (Chapter II). He resents Kurtz so much that he seems to be willing to let the trade suffer by sabotaging him. Marlow hints that he intentionally sank the steamer so that Kurtz, already ill, would die before help reached the Inner Station.

So his blandness conceals a deeper malignancy, which becomes most apparent as he watches Kurtz's slow death with satisfaction: "the 'affair' had come off as well as could be wished" (Chapter III). He half-starves the boat's African crew by refusing to stop to let them trade for food on shore. (He has plenty of his own.)

Unlike Kurtz, he can exercise restraint: "He was just the kind of man who would wish to preserve appearances. That was his restraint" (Chapter II). He cares a lot more about the appearance of being an upright manager than about the actual wrongs he commits. His crimes have the approval of society— most of them just involve carrying on the business of the big bureaucratic death-machine known as the Company.

Incidentally, the manager is based on the real-life Camille Delcommune, manager of a Congo trading station at which Conrad was stationed in much the same capacity as Marlow. He wrote to his aunt (September 26, 1890): "The manager is a common ivory-dealer with sordid instincts who considers himself a merchant though he is only a kind of African shop-keeper. His name is Delcommune. . . . I can hope for neither promotion nor increase of salary while he remains here." The dislike was mutual, so we can be sure that the portrait of the rotten manager is at least partly an act of revenge.

The Brickmaker

The brickmaker of the Central Station takes Marlow aside and tries to pump him for information under the mistaken impression that Marlow has highly influential connections in Europe. He would seem like more of a villain if he weren't so pathetically ineffective—as Marlow observes, he can't even manage to make bricks. (His attempt to get information from Marlow is so obvious and incompetent that it's comical.) He is a young aristocrat who toadies shamelessly to the manager, doing his menial secretarial tasks. The alliance has brought him a few special privileges, and also the dislike of the other pilgrims, who think he's the manager's spy. He's capable, as he demonstrates with Marlow, of fawning one minute and making veiled threats the next. Like his ally the manager, he resents Kurtz because he fears that if the highly efficient Kurtz is promoted to general manager, his own position will be endangered. The brickmaker is typical of the malaise that cripples all the Company's trading stations. Instead of a "devotion to efficiency" (which Marlow says early on is the saving grace of colonialism), he's devoted to himself. Trade and progress concern him a lot less than a possible promotion.

The Accountant

On first arriving at the Outer Station, Marlow becomes acquainted with the Company's chief accountant for Africa, a man who, in his "devotion to efficiency," is the very opposite of the brickmaker and the other pilgrims of the Central Station. His books are in "apple-pie order," and he really does care about his job, just as he cares about his appearance, which is immaculate. Marlow admires him. Further, the accountant thinks highly of Kurtz. After all, such an efficient worker would have no reason to fear for his job (unlike the manager and the brickmaker) if Kurtz were promoted, which he calmly predicts is what will happen. He holds the rest of the agents of the Central Station in little regard, and even suggests that to send Kurtz a letter through there would be imprudent because the agents there might snoop into it.

However, the accountant's devotion to efficiency blinds him to the sufferings of both whites and blacks in Africa. When a sick agent is brought into his office, he complains that the groans distract him from his work; he is not particularly concerned that the man is dying. He hates the Africans "to the death" simply because they make noise. Perhaps Conrad is suggesting—though not explicitly—that even at its best the Company is inhumane, caring more about numbers than about people. When Marlow last sees the accountant, he tells us he is "bent over his books, . . . making correct entries of perfectly correct transactions; and fifty feet below the doorstep I could see the still tree-tops of the grove of death" where a group of exhausted natives have crawled to die (Chapter I). "Perfectly correct transactions" is an ironic way of phrasing it. How could transactions that lead to wholesale death be perfectly correct?

Kurtz's Intended

Marlow meets the woman Kurtz was engaged to marry, his Intended (it is always capitalized), after Kurtz has been dead for more than a year. She is living under the delusion that Kurtz was generous, kind, and noble to the end, and Marlow doesn't choose to enlighten her. He lies that Kurtz died with her name on his lips. (Proper Victorian that he is, Marlow thinks it fitting and just that women be relegated to the world of "beautiful illusions.") But he pays a price for his dishonesty. The sudden recognition of how intimately goodness and lies are mingled in the world almost drives him to despair.

Though there's something saintly about the Intended, there's also something slightly repellent in the intensity of her delusion. She's linked by a gesture to Kurtz's savage mistress. And just as that woman represents the soul of the jungle in all its cruelty, the Intended is the soul of civilization, a civilization woven partly of truth and partly of the lies we need to go on living. The Belgian public needs the lie of the Company's high ideals and philanthropic intentions in order to stomach the colonization of the Congo; likewise, the Intended needs the lie of Kurtz's ideals and intentions to believe that he died for a worthwhile cause. But as Marlow perceives how necessary it is to lie, Kurtz's final judgment—"The horror! The horror!"—rings in his ears, and it suddenly seems like a judgment not just on Kurtz's own life and the darkness of Africa, but a judgment on even the best, the most beautiful parts of civilization—including the drawing room of this loyal, tragic woman.

Kurtz's Mistress

Talking of Kurtz, Marlow says that the wilderness had "loved him, embraced him" (Chapter II), and Conrad gives us a vivid symbol of that embrace in Kurtz's savage mistress. Marlow calls her the soul of the jungle—"wild and gorgeous," "savage and superb," and like the jungle, dangerous. She seems to be a leader of Kurtz's army; at least, she's the most fearless of his followers, the only one not petrified by the shriek of the steam whistle. As the boat departs, Marlow reports she "stretched tragically her bare arms after us over the sombre and glittering river" (Chapter III); and it's this gesture that reminds Marlow of her when he sees the Intended "put out her arms as if after a retreating figure . . . across the fading and narrowing sheen of the window" in her drawing room. One woman represents the civilization that loses Kurtz; the other symbolizes the jungle that destroys him.

The Pilgrims

The "pilgrims," as Marlow sarcastically calls them, are the 20 or so agents at the Central Station who carry long staves like actual religious travelers and talk so much about ivory that "You would think they were praying to it." Lazy and self-satisfied, they represent the worst of the whites in Africa: "as to effectually lifting a little finger—oh, no" (Chapter I). At one of the Congo trading stations Conrad visited, he recorded in his diary: "Prominent characteristic of the social life here; people speaking ill of each other." He must have been remembering this behavior when he wrote that the pilgrims "beguiled the time by backbiting and intriguing against each other in a foolish kind of way" (Chapter I). Although he despises them, Conrad uses the pilgrims for comic relief, especially on the trip upriver. (Three or four of them accompany Marlow and the manager.) During the attack, their terror and their wild gunfire are incongruously funny. But the pilgrims are also bloodthirsty; they enjoy massacring Africans. "Don't! don't you frighten them away," they cry when Marlow scares off their human targets with the screech of the steam whistle (Chapter III).

The Cannibals

On the trip upriver Marlow enlists a crew of about 30 cannibals to do the boat's manual labor. In contrast to the idiotic pilgrims, Conrad portrays the cannibals with dignity. They grow increasingly hungry on board, especially after the pilgrims throw their provision of stinking hippo meat overboard and the manager refuses to stop to trade for food on shore. Marlow tries to imagine why they don't eat him and the pilgrims, and the only answer he can offer is the restraint he values so highly in civilized people: "Restraint! I would just as soon have expected restraint from a hyena prowling amongst the corpses of a battlefield. But there was the fact facing me" (Chapter II). Marlow respects them: "They were men one could work with, and I am grateful to them." Work is one of Marlow's highest values, and the pilgrims, we know, are terrible workers. In fact, the pilgrims are always behaving on a level beneath what you would expect of civilized men, while the cannibals keep acting on a level above what you would expect of savages

The Fireman

The fireman is an African who has been trained to operate the boat's vertical boiler. Marlow says, ironically, that through instruction he's an "improved specimen," but he doesn't really understand the machine—he thinks there's an evil spirit inside who gets angry if you don't give him enough water. The fireman is an expression of Conrad's pessimism about civilizing the jungle. It can be done—perhaps—but it will be a long, slow process, much more difficult than all the glib, idealistic talk about "weaning those ignorant millions from their horrid ways" (Chapter I) takes account of.

The Helmsman

The African helmsman who steers the boat is an "athletic black belonging to some coast tribe" who dies from a spear wound during the attack on the steamer. He's a poor worker, swaggering and undependable, and Marlow (who calls him a fool) has to watch over him constantly. His death is largely his own fault, since he abandons his post to stand at the window and shoot wildly at the attacking tribe. "He had no restraint," Marlow comments, "no restraint—just like Kurtz" (Chapter II). Nevertheless, Marlow clearly values him. A subtle bond has grown between them through working together (Marlow is always thinking about the rewards of work), and he doesn't think getting to Kurtz was worth the death of his helmsman.

The Manager's Uncle

The manager's uncle arrives at the Central Station while Marlow is delayed there repairing his boat. He's a short, fat man who heads something called the Eldorado Exploring Expedition—a group pretending to be interested in geography but really just out to get rich. Marlow compares them to burglars. He also overhears a conversation between the manager and his uncle in which the uncle proves to be particularly bloodthirsty, urging his nephew to exercise his authority and hang whomever he wants to.

The Boiler-maker

Marlow's foreman is a mechanic at the Central Station, a boiler-maker by trade. His rough manners make him an object of disdain to the pilgrims, but he appeals to Marlow because of his capacity and enthusiasm for work. He makes only a brief appearance, just after Marlow's long talk with the brickmaker. His simple bluntness is a relief after the brickmaker's caginess, and his unrefined, working-class bearing forms an effective contrast to the brickmaker's effete, upper-class smugness.

Marlow's Aunt

Marlow's aunt is based, at least in part, on Marguerite Poradowska, who was related to Conrad by marriage. (She was not a true aunt, but he addressed her that way in his letters.) Like Marlow's aunt, Poradowska lived in Brussels and intervened on Conrad's behalf to secure him an appointment as captain of a Congo steamer.

If Conrad was trying to depict Marguerite Poradowska realistically, the portrait was not a very flattering one. The aunt has been swayed by all the "rot let loose in print and talk just about that time," and she prattles about the high (and false) ideals she's been hearing about—civilizing the ignorant masses, and so forth—until finally Marlow has to remind her that the Company is run for profit. Her chatter prompts the first of several passages on "how out of touch with truth women are" (Chapter I)—a reflection that comes home during Marlow's encounter with Kurtz's Intended at the end of the novel.

The Narrator

We learn very little about the actual narrator of the novel, the man who, aboard the *Nellie* anchored at the mouth of the Thames, hears Marlow spin his yarn and later reports it to us. But we can see that he has been affected by what he hears, as the change in imagery from the beginning to the end of the book indicates. At the outset he's impressed by all the light on the Thames, and he thinks about English nautical history in terms of light—for instance, "bearers of a spark from the sacred fire." By the end, his imagination is full of darkness. If Marlow intends his tale as a warning that we need to pay more heed to the "darkness"—the incomprehensible, the opposite of civilization and progress—then in the case of the narrator, at least, he's made his point.

Other Elements

SETTING

Although most of the action in *Heart of Darkness* is set in the jungles of the African Congo, the tale itself is narrated by a sailor aboard a pleasure boat at the mouth of the Thames River outside London. Both the time of day and the spot are significant. It's sunset; as the tale turns gloomier, images of darkness get more and more pervasive. The evening grows gradually darker, so that by the time Marlow finishes, late in the night, his listeners have literally been enveloped in darkness. The setting right outside London would put them next to the great seat of civilization (for an English novelist, at least)—a strategic place from which to hear a tale of the wilderness. In fact, for an English sailor the mouth of the Thames would mark the point between the light of civilization and the unknown ends of the earth. But by the end Marlow has made it clear that the "darkness" he is talking about has almost as much to do with the city as with the jungle.

Marlow's adventure takes place in the Congo Free State, an area that at the time was the personal property of Leopold II, king of the Belgians. There had been a lot of empty talk about Leopold's philanthropic and civilizing activities in the Congo, but by 1899, when *Heart of Darkness* first appeared, the grim conditions that actually prevailed there and the grotesquely inhumane treatment of the African natives were becoming widely enough known to create an international scandal. Conrad, who served as skipper of a Congo steamer himself in 1890, knew the true conditions, and much of the gruesome detail is drawn from observation. But he exaggerated a few points for literary purposes. Specifically, the Congo was already far more tamed by Conrad's time than the novel suggests. The river was dotted with active trading stations, and the station that would have been the equivalent of Kurtz's Inner Station had a number of company agents, not just one. Conrad's departures from the reality serve to emphasize the isolation of his characters, and thus to intensify the theme of solitude.

THEME

The darkness of the title is the major theme of the book, but the meaning of that darkness is never clearly defined. On the whole it stands for the unknown and the unknowable; it represents the opposite of the progress and enlightenment that dominated the 19th century. Not many years before, it had been widely believed that science was eventually going to cure the ills of the world; but by the end of the century a deeper pessimism had taken hold, and the darkness is Conrad's image for everything he most dreaded. Science had turned out to be a sham, at least as a route to human happiness—the world wasn't getting any better. Was the darkness something that was simply a part of the universe, something that could never be defeated? Or did it come from within human beings? The "heart of darkness" stands for many things—the interior of the jungle, the Inner Station, Kurtz's own black heart, perhaps the heart of every human being.

Conrad leaves the meanings of this darkness hazy on purpose. As the narrator tells us, for Marlow "the meaning of an episode was not inside like a kernel but outside, enveloping the tale which brought it out only as a glow brings out a haze" (Chapter I). He also calls the story "inconclusive." In other words, you can't easily reduce the meaning to a couple of sentences. Conrad doesn't declare—he hints and suggests. This quality sometimes makes it difficult to put your finger on exactly what it is about a passage that disturbs or moves or excites you, and it makes it difficult to explain the full meaning of certain symbols—especially the darkness. But it's exactly this quality that makes the book so creepy and unsettling that it lingers in the mind.

There are several running subthemes that you should note. Foremost among these is the notion of work. Whatever the darkness is, the best way to fend it off, and to stay sane, is by working. Conrad doesn't pretend that work is enjoyable, but it strengthens your character and makes you less likely to lose your grip in difficult situations. (One reason most of the white characters in the novel are so unattractive is that they don't do their work.) Another value he holds in esteem is restraint. Self-restraint takes determination, but it may save you from the grim consequences of thoughtless action. Conrad shows us two unsettling examples of individuals who lack restraint. One is the black helmsman on Marlow's boat; his inability to restrain himself leads to his death. The other example is Mr. Kurtz, whose lack of restraint is to a large degree the subject of the plot.

Another running theme could be called the unreliability of high ideals, or simply of words. (This is surprising from a novelist who's so verbose himself.) Conrad and his alter ego, Marlow, don't trust words. Actions are what you have to judge people by: actions can't lie, but words can. A related topic is the theme of illusions, and of delusions. Conrad believes that some illusions are necessary, especially for his women characters. But how necessary? And is a lie excusable, or even commendable, when it supports such an illusion?

STYLE

Since Marlow's tale is told aloud, Conrad makes his prose resemble a speaking voice. Thus we get pauses, hesitations, repetitions, digressions—all of which we normally associate with a speaker, not a writer. You get the sense of Marlow being at times completely absorbed by his memories, at others becoming abstracted and letting his mind wander; of his constantly trying to understand the meaning of his own tale. He is remarkably (sometimes painfully) wordy, testing a formulation, then backing off and trying another, until he's reached one he feels satisfied with. It's almost as if he wants to trap his worst memories in a soft cocoon of words.

Conrad's so-called impressionist method lets us experience Marlow's sensations along with him. The author mounts detail on detail before finally putting them all together to find their significance. For example, at the Inner Station where Marlow has gone to retrieve Kurtz, he spies six posts with ornamental balls on top and assumes that they must be the remainder of some kind of fence. Later, looking through a telescope, the balls come into focus and he realizes they're human heads. We experience his misperception as well as his sudden revelation, and even the revelation comes in stages: first his surprise—"its first result was to make me throw my head back as if before a blow" (Chapter III)—and then his deduction. So we take part in the mental process. This kind of immediacy, this emphasis on sensation, makes the jungle seem very real, and it's particularly effective during such episodes as the attack on the steamer.

But it has a further implication. The emphasis is on what you can know with your senses—these facts are reliable. Marlow, of course, is constantly examining his sensations to find the meaning in them, expressing opinions and doubts, but seldom coming to firm conclusions. Marlow's experiences, as the narrator tells us (Chapter I), are "inconclusive," and for such inconclusiveness Conrad's impressionist style is appropriate.

POINT OF VIEW

Marlow is clearly Conrad's alter ego; his opinions don't differ significantly from what we know about the author's own. But Marlow has tremendous importance as a literary device. By using an actual speaking sailor to tell the story, Conrad goes just about as far away as you can get from the typical 19th-century novel's omniscient narrator—the all-knowing voice of an impersonal author who told you not only what happened to the characters but also what went on in their minds. We're never allowed to know more than Marlow himself, and Marlow knows only what he perceives through his senses. Thus, we're never directly told what motivated, say, the manager or Kurtz. Instead, we get Marlow's speculations on what their motivations might have been.

What's most unusual about the point of view in *Heart of Darkness* isn't the use of Marlow as narrator, but that his tale is framed by the narration of another, nameless observer. As a result, Marlow's whole story appears somewhat cumbersomely enclosed in quotation marks. Why couldn't Conrad just make Marlow the primary narrator and drop the nameless voice at the beginning and the end?

One reason is that by having Marlow in front of us on the cruising yawl *Nellie*, we feel the immediacy of his speaking voice, we get the actual sensation of a crusty sailor spinning a yarn before us. If Conrad had written the whole novel in the first person, dispensing with the primary narrator, he'd have ended up with a more "writerly" book, in which Marlow's hesitations and digressions—which are such an important element in the style—would have no place. We would also miss the feeling that Marlow was working out the meaning of his tale as he went along, and that we were a part of that process. A writer, unlike a talker, usually has things worked out beforehand.

The meaning of the novel lies not only in what happened in Africa, but also in Marlow's conviction that he has to tell others about these events as a kind of warning. The representative Victorians aboard the *Nellie* need to be told about the threat of the darkness, the threat to progress and enlightenment, because for the most part the Victorian world hadn't acknowledged that threat. By putting his audience, especially the primary narrator, on the deck of the *Nellie* with Marlow, Conrad emphasizes this warning aspect of Marlow's tale—and its effect on his listeners.

FORM AND STRUCTURE

Heart of Darkness is structured as a journey of discovery, both externally in the jungle, and internally in Marlow's own mind. The deeper he penetrates into the heart of the jungle, the deeper he delves within himself; by the climax, when Kurtz has been revealed for the disgrace he is, Marlow has also learned something about himself. And he returns to civilization with this new knowledge.

Formally, *Heart of Darkness* looks forward to many of the developments of the modern novel—most notably the fracturing of time. Marlow doesn't tell his tale straight through from beginning to end; he'll skip from an early event to a late event and back again. Thus, we get several pages about Kurtz—Marlow's impressions and evaluation of his behavior—close to the end of Chapter II, but Kurtz himself doesn't appear on the scene until some way into Chapter III. Nor would a typical 19th-century narrator interrupt a buildup of suspense like the depiction of the boat waiting to be attacked in the fog with a lengthy digression on cannibalism and self-restraint. But Marlow does. He's describing the fog and the fright of the white pilgrims on board, which leads him to recall the reactions of the black Africans on board, and suddenly he's off on a tangent about cannibalism that brings the development of the action to a complete halt. In a more traditional novel this passage would have been reserved for a more appropriate place, for example, when the author first introduced the cannibals. But Marlow imparts his thoughts as they occur to him. Conrad was trying to find a form that more closely followed the contours of human thought—a less artificial form than the traditional novel. (Later novelists, notably James Joyce and William Faulkner, took these experiments with fractured time and space much further.) Hence the forward and backward leaps, the interruptions, the thoughts left dangling.

The Story

Conrad divided *Heart of Darkness* into three longish chapters. To make discussion easier, they can be subdivided as follows:

CHAPTER I
1. Prologue: Marlow Begins His Tale.
2. The Sepulchral City. The Company.
3. Africa. The Outer Station.
4. The Trek. The Central Station.
5. The Brickmaker.
6. The Boiler-maker. The Eldorado Expedition.

CHAPTER II
1. The Manager and His Uncle.
2. The Journey Upriver.
3. The Message. The Fog. Cannibals.
4. The Attack.
5. Kurtz.
6. The Inner Station.

CHAPTER III
1. The Russian's Story.
2. Kurtz. His Mistress. Departure of the Russian.
3. Kurtz's Escape. Departure.
4. Kurtz's Death.
5. Marlow's Illness and Return.
6. The Lie.
7. Epilogue.

Be sure to note that these subdivisions aren't Conrad's. They are used in this guide only to make the novel easier to analyze and discuss.

Quotations cited can usually be found in the subdivision being discussed. When a quotation is from a subdivision other than the one under discussion, it will be identified this way: "(III, 5)", meaning Chapter III, subdivision 5—the subdivision titled "Marlow's Illness and Return."

CHAPTER I

PROLOGUE: MARLOW BEGINS HIS TALE

Five Englishmen are enjoying themselves one pleasant afternoon aboard a sailboat close to the mouth of the Thames River outside London. Since there isn't much wind, they're stranded when the tide turns ("The flood had made"); all they can do is drop anchor and wait several hours until the tide shifts again. The men on board are our nameless narrator; a weathered sailor by the name of Marlow; and three typical representatives of Victorian professional society: a lawyer, an accountant, and a director of companies (who owns the boat).

Sunset: the light on the Thames is brilliant. Our narrator patriotically recalls the great British sailors, from the 16th-century Sir Francis Drake to the 19th-century Sir John Franklin, who navigated this river in times past. His thoughts are full of satisfaction and nationalistic smugness: these heroes, he reflects, are "bearers of a spark from the sacred fire" of English civilization.

NOTE: The narrator exhibits an optimism that was typical of the Victorians: he thinks civilization (particularly British civilization) is going to make the world better and better. It was widely believed in the 19th century that scientific and technological progress would eventually turn the world into a paradise. We can sense something of this attitude in our narrator's enthusiastic tone, and it's probable that his three professional companions share his viewpoint. We never learn much about these men individually, but Conrad may have chosen them to represent the Victorian bourgeoisie—that optimistic class to whom Marlow's warning tale will be largely addressed. These people believed smugly that enlightenment would overcome backwardness; in terms of images, that light (as in "enlightenment") was bound to conquer the darkness of ignorance and superstition.

Notice how our primary narrator's descriptions sparkle with images of light: he believes, too confidently, in the forces of progress. The cautionary tale he's about to hear about a journey into the "heart of darkness" is going to dampen some of this easy confidence.

NOTE: Be sure to pay particular attention at this point to the images of light on the river, because they'll form an important contrast to the book's closing images of darkness. In fact, this contrast will make up the most pervasive image pattern in the novel. You should keep an eye out for the way Conrad uses light and dark, or white and black, for much of the novel's meaning can be deduced from these image patterns.

The men are sitting in silence when, out of the blue, Marlow observes that the very civilized land around them was once a primitive wilderness, "one of the dark places of the earth." He imagines how ominously ancient England must have struck its Roman conquerors. The savage land must have seemed horrible to any civilized Roman commander. Marlow describes the way the "fascination of the abomination" of a place like that might go to work unhinging the mind of such a man. Although Marlow seems to be rambling, Conrad is actually foreshadowing what is going to happen later in the book. The tale Marlow tells will concern a modern-day colonizer, Mr. Kurtz, who succumbs to "the fascination of the abomination" in the wilderness of Africa. The phrase is only vaguely ominous now, but its meaning will grow clearer as Marlow develops his tale.

Nevertheless, Marlow continues, there wasn't much to admire in these Roman conquerors. They were really just glorified robbers out to get whatever they could grab. In fact, the conquest of the earth is an ugly thing—greed carried out on a large scale. But, he adds, it can be redeemed by a "devotion to efficiency" and by an idea—the idea of progress. Conquest for plunder is one thing, but conquest for the purpose of civilizing the world is something else entirely.

Again, through this seemingly casual monologue Conrad is introducing another major theme: the brutality of colonization. But observe that as scathing as Marlow is about brute conquest, he makes an exception for those conquerors who spread progress and enlightenment around the globe, which was exactly how the British saw themselves.

NOTE: Conrad probably put these positive sentiments about colonization into Marlow's mouth in order to pacify his British audience. Britain at that time, after all, was one of the great imperial powers, and British readers wouldn't have taken kindly to an out-and-out attack on the morality of colonization.

Marlow's reflections remind him of an incident in his own past, and the narrator realizes that he's about to launch into a tale.

THE SEPULCHRAL CITY. THE COMPANY

As a boy, Marlow tells the group, he used to be fascinated by maps, especially the blank spaces—places that hadn't yet been explored. (This was true of the young Conrad, too.) At the start of his tale he's a young sailor just back from a stint in the Orient, and looking without much success for work. One day in a shop window he sees a map of the African Congo—one of the blank spaces of his childhood maps and hardly more explored now. The trading companies on the Congo River, he realizes, must use steamboats; it dawns on him that he could get a commission as skipper of one of them.

Since the Congo Free State was a possession of the king of the Belgians, Leopold II, Marlow asks an influential aunt who lives in Brussels to try to help him get a post. She succeeds; a new captain is needed to replace the skipper of one of the Company's boats, who was killed in a scuffle with the Africans.

NOTE: From 1885 to 1908 the Congo Free State, a territory of almost one million square miles, was the personal property of Leopold II. Leopold spoke in the most exalted terms about civilizing the Africans, yet the exploitation, massacre, and enslavement of the natives got worse with each year of his reign. *Heart of*

Darkness was one of the early expressions of a revulsion that eventually grew to international proportions.

Marlow's nickname for Brussels, "the sepulchral city," comes from the words of Jesus (Matthew 23:27–28): "Woe unto you, scribes and Pharisees, hypocrites! for ye are like unto whited sepulchres [tombs], which indeed appear beautiful outward, but are within full of dead men's bones, and of all uncleanness. Even so ye also outwardly appear righteous unto men, but within ye are full of hypocrisy and iniquity." This would make a good description of the Belgians' hypocrisy toward the Congo: they claimed to be guiding and helping the Africans, when in fact they were enslaving and slaughtering them in record numbers.

NOTE: Marlow never calls Brussels by name, nor, for that matter, does he name the Company, the Congo, the Congo River, or most of the characters in the novel. Conrad once wrote that explicitness "is fatal to the glamour of all artistic work, robbing it of all suggestiveness, destroying all illusion." Because unnamed cities and characters seem more general, they can carry a heavier burden of symbolic meaning—and Conrad wanted to load his novel with symbolic meaning.

Marlow visits the offices of "the Company" that has a large concession in the Congo. They strike him as ominous, disturbing. Two women sit in the outer office, dressed in black and knitting black wool. Marlow fancifully imagines greeting them with the cry of the Roman gladiators. The phrase, in Latin, translates

as "Hail! We who are about to die salute you!"—
which wouldn't be altogether wrong, since more than
half of those who traveled to the Congo never came
back. After being introduced briefly to the director of
the Company, Marlow is accompanied by a clerk to
his medical examination. The clerk prattles about the
glories of the Company's business, but when Marlow
asks him why he himself hasn't traveled to Africa, he
suddenly turns cold and intimates that only a fool
would go there. The doctor isn't very reassuring,
either. He keeps hinting (though he never says so
directly) that if Marlow goes to Africa he may go mad,
and he offers the not-very-helpful advice that he
should try to "avoid irritation" there. Madness is
indeed a terror Marlow will face—and nearly succumb to—in the jungle, but as yet he doesn't know
why, though he has an inkling that something isn't
right.

NOTE: Conrad has created an ominous atmosphere
before Marlow even leaves for Africa. The Congo
River on a map looks like a snake to Marlow, and you
don't have to recall that ever since the story of what
happened in the Garden of Eden the snake has been a
symbol of evil to sense the reason that this image
bodes ill for Marlow. He comes right out and says that
"it fascinated me as a snake would a bird—a silly little
bird." Will it, in some sense, swallow him up, make
him its own? Likewise, the Company's offices are
gloomy and strange, and its officials behave as if they
were all in on some evil secret. And in a sense they
are: the secret is the horrible brutality of the Belgians
to the black Africans. Marlow isn't naïve, but he isn't
prepared for the terrible spectacle that will confront
him when he gets to the Congo.

Before leaving "the sepulchral city" of Brussels, Marlow pays a visit to the aunt who helped get him his commission. Talking to her he realizes that she must have recommended him not merely as a good sailor but as an exceptional and gifted man as well. He's embarrassed not only because of his natural modesty but, more to the point, because he perceives that he's expected to travel down as an "emissary of light"—an apostle of civilization in the jungle, spreading enlightenment among the ignorant millions. All this rhetoric—the "rot let loose in print and talk just about that time," he calls it—strikes him as hypocritical, and he's disturbed to hear his aunt spouting it.

NOTE: This discrepancy between the myths and the facts—the unreliability of words—will form one of Conrad's major themes.

Marlow is unable to make his aunt see the truth. Women, he reflects condescendingly, live in a world of beautiful illusions. Marlow's opinions about women strike us as offensive today, but they wouldn't have seemed unusual to Conrad's Victorian audience, which regarded its women—at least its wealthy ones—as fragile creatures who needed to be protected from life and work. (Work, we'll find, is one of Marlow's highest values.) In any case, the passage is an important one; you should keep it in mind when you reach the last scene of Marlow's tale, in which he confronts another woman, a woman whose illusions won't seem so beautiful.

AFRICA. THE OUTER STATION

From the beginning, Africa creates an unsettling impression for Marlow. For example, he watches a battleship firing its guns at the overgrown bank; the ship seems tiny and helpless against the immensity of the jungle, almost as if it were attempting to fire not at men but at a continent. The image gives us a sense of the littleness of human beings against the immensity of the jungle; it suggests that conquering the jungle is a task so tremendous that it's almost hopeless.

The sailors on board that French ship, Marlow learns, are dying at the rate of three a day. Disease was then the greatest hazard one faced in Africa. Conrad, too, came down with dysentery during his journey to the Congo; and Marlow himself will face a bout of fever before the end.

A Swedish captain takes Marlow from the mouth of the Congo upstream to the Company's Outer Station. Talking to Marlow the Englishman, this captain seems contemptuous of the Belgian officials there. He, too, seems to suggest that the jungle is a stronger opponent than most Europeans think; and he hints that it can drive you mad, mentioning another man he recently brought upriver, who ended up hanging himself.

When Marlow reaches the Outer Station he's appalled by practically everything he finds there. The place is a nightmare of disorder and inefficiency. Machinery is rusting in the grass; a shipment of imported pipes lies smashed at the bottom of a ravine. A cliff wall is being dynamited to make way for a railroad (even though it doesn't seem to Marlow to be in the way of anything) but the explosion seems to have no effect at all on the rock. Again, the jungle—so romantic and unthreatening when Marlow envisioned it back in London—now seems so immense, so powerful, that the white man's puny efforts to bring order into it look pathetic.

Marlow hears a clinking noise and he turns to see a chain gang of raggedy, emaciated blacks, iron collars around their necks. This gruesome vision disgusts Marlow, and he moves aside to let them get ahead and out of sight.

NOTE: These men are our first view of the brutality that will form so much a part of Marlow's Congo experience: they are criminals according to a set of European laws that they could never hope to understand. They're followed by a self-important African guard who doesn't understand any better.

But he's about to witness something even more terrible. He steps down into a gloomy grove and discovers a group of dying Africans. These men aren't legally criminals or slaves either, though they're bound by "time contracts" to work for set periods. They certainly don't understand contracts and probably don't even understand time. These victims are workers who have become diseased and worn out, maybe because of the unfamiliar food or the unpleasant surroundings far from their homes. So they're allowed to crawl away and die. They're a perfect, vivid emblem of what the white man has done to the black man in Africa. For his part, Marlow is horrified. Glancing down, he sees a face near his hand; he reaches nervously into his pocket and comes out with a cracker. Marlow's description of his gesture is typically self-effacing; he isn't given to celebrating his own virtues. As a gesture of compassion, his action may not seem like much, but it surpasses anything we're going to see from the other white men in the novel, who don't even seem to perceive the Africans as human.

Marlow has had enough. He climbs uphill to the Station's main buildings. Soon he encounters a character who seems to embody the very opposite of all the disorder, ugliness, and futility he's seen so far. The man is wearing snowy white trousers, a light jacket, and polished boots; he has carefully brushed and parted his hair and he's holding a parasol to protect his skin from the sun. He turns out to be the Companys' chief accountant. Before long Marlow has a chance to observe him at his job, and he's impressed with the precision and neatness with which he manages his paperwork, just as he's impressed with the appearance that he manages to keep up in the middle of such confusion. He's the only example we've seen of the "devotion to efficiency" that Marlow said (I, 1) was the only excuse for colonization.

But the chief accountant is so fanatically devoted to efficiency in the form of neatness and precision that it becomes hard to admire or even like him. When one of the Company's agents is brought into his office to lie out of the sun, he shows no interest or sympathy, though the agent is feverish, delirious, and apparently at death's door. In fact, he complains that the man's groans make it difficult for him to concentrate on his work. When the Africans outside raise a shout about something, he tells Marlow that the distractions they create have made him "hate them to the death." The chief accountant understands the values of the numbers in his ledger books better than he understands the value of a life. If he exhibits virtues of orderliness that most of the Belgian colonizers utterly lack, he also shares a common failing with them: a lack of compassion, of feeling, of respect for life.

One day the accountant mentions a certain Mr. Kurtz, whom Marlow will no doubt meet upriver. When Marlow inquires about this Kurtz, the accountant tells him that he's a remarkable agent of the Company. From his post at the Inner Station (about one thousand miles away, we later learn), he's managed to send back more ivory than all the other agents combined. Apparently he has a high reputation in the Company's European office; the accountant is sure that he's going to be promoted into the administration soon, and that "he will go far, very far."

NOTE: This is the first mention of a character who will become pivotal to Marlow's tale. At this point he's only the vague form of an efficient agent. But as Marlow gets closer and closer to the Inner Station, Mr. Kurtz will sharpen into grim focus.

THE TREK. THE CENTRAL STATION

To get from the Outer Station to the Company's Central Station 200 miles inland, Marlow has to make a difficult overland trek. He's accompanied by a fat and sickly trader and a crew of 60 black carriers.

The path they travel is strangely deserted. Of course, Marlow reflects, if the English countryside suddenly filled with a lot of mysterious blacks armed with fearful weapons, who went around capturing the locals and forcing them to carry heavy loads, it would probably clear out pretty quickly, too. It's basically just a comic observation; but, again, it shows an empathy in Marlow that the other whites don't share. Even though his tone is flip, he makes a connection between the lives of Africans and the lives of his compatriots that would never occur to his white colleagues.

The party encounters a white officer who claims his job is keeping the road up (though, as far as Marlow can see, there isn't any road); nearby, they find the corpse of an African, a bullet hole through his forehead. The trip turns even more unpleasant when the fat white trader becomes ill. Unfit for the hardships of such a hike, he's constantly fainting. (When Marlow asks him why he ever came to Africa he replies scornfully, "To make money, of course"—one more greedy white.) Eventually he comes down with a fever and has to be carried in a hammock. He's so fat that some of the crew sneak away at night to get out of having to lug him. One evening Marlow lectures them sternly, and the next day he sends the hammock with its carriers off in front. An hour later he finds it overturned in a bush, its furious cargo groaning and demanding somebody's death. Marlow remembers a remark of the doctor in Brussels (the one who told him to avoid irritation, which he is not managing to do) that it would be interesting to watch the "mental changes" of individuals who went to Africa. "I felt I was becoming scientifically interesting," Marlow says drily. Again, the tone is slightly comic, but the spectre of madness had already begun to show itself—faintly.

After 15 days they finally reach the Central Station, which turns out to be just as disorganized and disorderly as the Outer Station. One of the agents immediately tells Marlow that the steamship he was supposed to command is lying at the bottom of the river.

Before he has any time to rest from his 20-mile walk that morning, Marlow is ushered in for an interview with the station's manager. He doesn't find much to like or admire in the man. The manager is a "common trader," common in learning, common in intelligence, and with no talent for administration and no ability to inspire the men he commands. In fact, his only real talent seems to be for staying healthy—no small advantage in country where whites are constantly coming down with deadly fevers.

As soon as Marlow walks in, the manager begins chattering about the wreck. You may realize only in retrospect how nervously he behaves, and it should make you suspicious. (Marlow isn't suspicious, though—yet.) The manager tells him he tried to set out two days before with a volunteer skipper, and almost immediately they tore out the bottom of the boat on stones. It sank at once. They just couldn't wait for Marlow any longer, the manager claims, they'd heard that an important station upriver was in danger and that its chief, Mr. Kurtz, was ill. Marlow tells him he's already heard of Kurtz. The manager is interested to learn that they speak of him at the Outer Station, and he quickly and rather nervously assures Marlow that Kurtz is their best agent, an important and exceptional man. He protests too much, as if he thinks Marlow has some reason to suspect him of lying.

Marlow, telling the story later, hints that the manager may not have been exactly honest about the wreck. "Certainly," Marlow says, "the affair was too stupid—when I think of it—to be altogether natural." The manager fidgets suspiciously, as if he had something to hide. We're going to find out later that he really hates Kurtz. Since he knows Kurtz is ill, there's good reason for us to suspect that he was willing to sabotage the steamboat in order to keep from having to save him. But suspect is all we can do; Marlow gives us no final evidence on the charge.

Note: Conrad didn't shape the incidents in the novel for literary and symbolic purposes alone. He was telling an exotic adventure story, and early readers were especially fascinated by the authentic descriptions of African ordeals. Conrad later wrote, in his author's note to the volume in which *Heart of Darkness* was published, that the novel was "authentic in fundamentals" and that it represented "experience pushed a little (and only a very little) beyond the actual facts of the case." You might be surprised at the number of incidents that Conrad *didn't* invent. The strenuous trek; the corpse of the shot native; the sickly companion; the carriers' resentment at having to haul him, and the speech to them; the wrecked steamer— all these details come straight from the pages of Conrad's Congo diary.

The manager, too, is drawn from life. he's based on the figure of Camille Delcommune, a local manager and official of the outfit for which Conrad worked in the Congo. For some reason Delcommune and Conrad took an intense dislike to each other, so Conrad was probably getting even when he drew the manager as such a repellent nothing of a character.

THE BRICKMAKER

To Marlow's disgust the other agents at the Central Station seem to spend most of their time either backbiting or wandering aimlessly around in the sun. With the long staffs they always carry, they remind him of "a lot of faithless pilgrims." A pilgrim is a traveler to a holy place; why should Marlow pick this word for the unholy agents? He supplies the answer himself: "The word 'ivory' rang in the air, was whispered, was sighed. You would think they were praying to it."

One evening a fire breaks out in one of the storage sheds, and the "pilgrims" run around idiotically trying to put it out. Marlow watches one of them attempt to fill a bucket that has a hole in the bottom—another moment of comedy, and another example of the gross incompetence that reigns at the Central Station. Meanwhile, he falls into conversation with one of the agents, a young aristocrat who's a flunky to the manager and a snob to the other agents. On their side, they think he's the manager's spy. How could these men ever conquer the wilderness when they can't even conquer their petty jealousies?

This man is supposed to be a brickmaker but, true to the inefficiency of the place, he hasn't managed to make any bricks because he lacks some material or other that he needs. The young man invites Marlow to his room, and as the two talk Marlow slowly realizes that the brickmaker is pumping him for information—even though he has no idea what useful information he might possess. The brickmaker drops a lot of hints about Marlow's connections in Brussels, and he gets more and more annoyed because he thinks Marlow is hiding something from him.

Marlow is struck by a painting in the room—a blindfolded woman carrying a lighted torch—and the brickmaker tells him that it was done by Mr. Kurtz when he was at the Central Station more than a year ago.

NOTE: The painting is obviously symbolic. The lighted torch reminds us of the primary narrator's description near the beginning of the novel of heroic British navigators: "bearing the sword, and often the torch, messengers of the might within the land, bearers of a spark from the sacred fire" (I, 1). The woman is carrying what must be the torch of enlightenment amid, we may surmise, the darkness of ignorance. But why should this emblem of colonization be blindfolded? Shouldn't colonizers enter the wilderness with their eyes open? (Obviously, from Marlow's experience so far, many of them haven't.) And why isn't the torch illuminating the "sombre—almost black" background as knowledge is supposed to enlighten ignorance? And finally, why does the torchlight have a "sinister" rather that an agreeable effect on the woman's face? Conrad doesn't place a heavy emphasis on this symbolic painting, and neither should we. But if you think about it you might find it a little disquieting. Does it mean that the forces of light have no hope of illuminating the darkness? Or is its significance more particular, a glimpse into the mind of Kurtz? And if Kurtz is the bearer of light (as, we'll see, he claims to be), is there something "sinister" about him?

Marlow asks for more information about Kurtz. The brickmaker tells him that Kurtz is "an emissary of pity and science and progress"—i.e., of light—one of the brilliant new breed who have come to Africa not just for profit, but with a higher mission to civilize the Africans. Kurtz is a special being, as Marlow ought to know. Marlow doesn't know why he ought to know, but the brickmaker won't let him get a word in. Right now, he continues, Kurtz is chief of the best station; next year he'll probably be assistant manager, and who knows how high he'll climb after that. He thinks Marlow ought to know because Marlow too is one of "the new gang—the gang of virtue." Suddenly everything becomes clear. Marlow recalls his aunt's claptrap about his being an "emissary of light" in the jungle, and he remembers the exceptional terms of praise she had used to recommend him. Word has somehow reached this young man, and he must think that Marlow is terribly influential with the Company's European office, and that he's in league with Kurtz. The brickmaker had planned to become assistant manager under the current manager; the arrival of the awesomely impressive Kurtz must have thrown a wrench into the plans of both men.

The brickmaker's rather confusing jabber about the "gang of virtue" refers to a conflict between King Leopold, who had a monopoly on trade in the Congo, and the private companies to which he had granted concessions, one of which is the so-called Company Marlow is working for. These companies found a propaganda advantage in allying themselves with the reformers who were genuinely interested in improving conditions for the Africans—they could claim to be doing some good beyond lining their own pockets. It was only a pose, but since it was the Company's official line, plenty of agents took it seriously, including Kurtz. Thus, the "gang of virtue" is the new wave of Company men professing the new ideals, and they threaten the entrenched positions of the old-school bureaucrats like the manager and the brickmaker.

So far Kurtz hasn't been much more than a word to Marlow. And yet now Marlow does something for this unknown quantity that's against all his principles, something that makes him feel miserable and sick: he lies for him. It isn't a gross lie, he just keeps quiet and lets the brickmaker go on thinking that he has a lot of influence in Europe. He can't even really explain the reason he does it, beyond saying that he had the impression that his lie would be helpful to Kurtz (apparently by keeping the brickmaker—and the manager—intimidated). Why should he be loyal to Kurtz? Because at this point he's heard nothing but praise for his efficiency and his high ideals, assets that are rare (to put it mildly) in the whites he's met so far.

NOTE: It's ironic that Marlow should do something counter to his principles in order to protect a man whose principles he admires, or thinks he admires. Nor is this the last time that Marlow, the hater of lies, is going to lie for Kurtz. He's destined, like it or not, to remain loyal to Kurtz, even after he learns more than he ever wanted to know about Kurtz and what Kurtz has turned into out there in the jungle.

The two men go outside, and the brickmaker becomes even oilier, calling Kurtz a "universal genius" and pitching himself as the kind of intelligent man who could be useful to him. He knows that Marlow is going to see Kurtz before he will, and he wants Marlow to put in a good word for him. He makes excuses for not making bricks, and for the menial secretarial work he performs for the manager: after all, it's only sensible to seek the confidence of your superiors. The man is obviously a shameless bootlicker who will try to curry favor with anybody he thinks can help him get ahead.

Marlow lets him run on for a while, but finally he tells him that what he really wants are rivets for repairing the steamboat. He hasn't been able to get any himself, but the brickmaker, he intimates, could get them for him if he set his mind to it. "My dear sir," the young man replies, "I write from dictation"— meaning that he's just a secretary, that only the manager has any real power to do favors for Marlow. Marlow insists that he could get them if he wanted. Offended, the brickmaker turns very cold and even, in a slimy way, menacing. He mentions a hippo that seems to have a charmed life, even though the pilgrims have emptied their rifles into it. But that can be said only about jungle beasts. "No man—you apprehend me?—no man here bears a charmed life," he tells Marlow, and on that outrageously (and unconvincingly) threatening note, this pathetically ineffectual man departs with a curt goodnight.

NOTE: Conrad has a particular metaphor for the spiritual emptiness of the white men in Africa, and it gains power every time he uses it. "Perhaps there was nothing within him," Marlow says of the manager (I, 4); and as he's talking to the brickmaker he observes, "It seemed to me that if I tried I could poke my fore-finger through him, and would find nothing inside but a little loose dirt, maybe." Later we will find out that Kurtz, too, "was hollow at the core" (III, 1). No wonder that T.S. Eliot called his 1925 poem on the subject of spiritual desolation "The Hollow Men," and chose an epigraph for it from *Heart of Darkness*.

THE BOILER-MAKER. THE ELDORADO EXPEDITION

Even though the brickmaker protested that he was powerless to help, Marlow thinks his request for riv-ets may have done some good. After all, the brick-maker still thinks that Marlow is an influential man, and he does want to get into his good graces. Marlow returns to the boat, which he's taken to staying with day and night (he even sleeps on it). There he talks with his foreman, a boiler-maker by trade. The fore-man is a rough, working-class mechanic, bald and bearded. He's disdained by the pilgrims, but Marlow admires him—after all, he *works*, as opposed to the pilgrims, who don't do much of anything.

NOTE: Marlow's comments on the subject of work would have struck a responsive chord in his Victorian audience. Work was one of the highest Victorian val-ues, and it's one of his own. He tells us that it's only through work that you find your own reality, that you learn what has real meaning for yourself. The subject of work is a running theme in the novel. Marlow touched on it during his opening monologue when he maintained that the "devotion to efficiency" is part of what redeems the excesses of colonization (I, 1). Later, on the river, Marlow's devotion to work (or to his boat, which comes to the same thing) will help to hold him back from the edge of madness.

When Marlow tells the boiler-maker that he may have succeeded in getting their rivets, the two men get as excited as children. They dance a jig on the deck of the boat and raise a tremendous clatter, which the jungle answers with its huge, unnerving silence. Marlow predicts that the rivets will come in three weeks.

But they don't come. What comes instead is a party of explorers—Marlow calls them "an invasion, an infliction"—named the Eldorado Exploring Expedition, and led by the manager's uncle. Eldorado was a mythical land of riches in South America. The Spanish conquistadors attempted to find it, and when they failed they ravaged the continent, leaving behind them a trail of conquest and misery. So "Eldorado" is the right name for the expedition: to Marlow, its members are just as disgusting and greedy as the other whites he's encountered so far. They've come to Africa "to tear the treasure out of the bowels of the land," and this desire to get rich, Marlow comments, "had no more moral purpose at the back of it than is in burglars breaking into a safe."

NOTE: The first chapter ends here (with another brief mention of the mysterious Kurtz), but the chapter breaks aren't really very significant. *Heart of Dark-*

ness first ran in three installments in *Blackwood's Edinburgh Magazine* (February, March, April 1899), so Conrad (or the editors) divided it into three roughly equal parts for serialization.

CHAPTER II

THE MANAGER AND HIS UNCLE

One evening as Marlow lies snoozing on the deck of his steamer, he's awakened by a conversation. The manager and his uncle are talking beside the boat; they don't realize Marlow's sleeping on top of it.

Conrad was trying here to capture the feel of a half-heard conversation. For that reason, you may find their talk a little hard to follow, especially at first. But it helps to know that the two men are talking about Kurtz. The manager, it appears, feels just as threatened by Kurtz as the brickmaker did: "Look at the influence that man must have," he tells his uncle. "Is it not frightful?" (The manager and the brickmaker are eager to attribute as much of their rival's success as they can to "influence"; it's easier to admit that he's more influential than that he's more talented than they are.) The uncle, in his turn, suggests callously that the climate may take care of the problem—with a little luck, Kurtz could die out there alone at the Inner Station. (We know already that he's rumored to be ill.) The manager is also irked about an insolent note Kurtz sent him. But Kurtz keeps sending back ivory, and lots of it, which impresses Company higher-ups, though it infuriates the manager.

Some months ago, we learn, Kurtz began his return trip on the river, with a clerk and a huge shipment of ivory. But 300 miles along the way he decided, for some reason, to turn back. The clerk, who brought the ivory the rest of the way to the Central Station, reported that Kurtz had been seriously ill and that he'd "recovered imperfectly." What could possibly have caused a sick man to return to a lonely outpost where there are no other civilized whites? Actually, Kurtz isn't the only white man at the station. We learn by putting together bits and pieces of the manager's talk that some sort of wandering trader is out there, too. The presence of a non-Company trader angers the manager still further: he calls him "unfair competiton" and declares that he ought to be hanged. The blood-thirsty uncle immediately agrees that the scoundrel *should* be hanged: "Anything—anything can be done in this country," he tells his nephew, meaning that out here in the wilderness the manager's word is law.

The manager goes on ranting about Kurtz. He's especially galled by the ideals Kurtz was always spouting when he was at the Central Station. "Each station," Kurtz had said, sounding very much like the "emissary of pity and science and progress" the brick-maker had called him (I, 5), "should be like a beacon" (note the image of light) "on the road toward better things, a centre for trade of course, but also for humanizing, improving, instructing." This prompts the manager to comment, "That ass!" to which he adds bitterly, "And he wants to be manager!" No wonder he feels threatened.

NOTE: What have we learned about Kurtz so far? Little by little we're getting hints that all isn't right with him. Since we know that he's ill and probably in need of medication, it's hard to explain why he would return to his lonely outpost. We've been told twice now—by the brickmaker and by the manager—that he's a man of the highest moral ideals; but we also know that he's living in a land with "no external checks" (I, 4), no laws, a land where, as the uncle declares, "anything can be done" if you have the authority of the gun. The question is: alone in the jungle, has Kurtz been able to stay loyal to his ideals?

The manager's own health has been "like a charm," but most of the agents who come to Africa, he says, sicken and die more quickly than he can send them out of the country. "Ah, my boy," the uncle reassures him once again, the jungle will take care of Kurtz. "Trust to this," he tells his nephew, and he points to the foreboding land—"to the lurking death, to the hidden evil, to the profound darkness of its heart. . . . The high stillness confronted these two figures with its ominous patience, waiting for the passing away of a fantastic invasion."

NOTE: Conrad invests the jungle with human qualities, as if it were some kind of patient monster waiting for the "fantastic invasion" of white men to pass— or waiting to pounce on them. This technique is called *personification*, and Conrad will use it throughout to portray the wilderness. By giving the dark jungle intelligence, and a certain malice, he achieves some of his creepiest effects.

The uncle's gesture toward the forest is so eerie and so startling that Marlow forgets himself and leaps to his feet on the boat. The noise scares the wits out of the two men, and after swearing from sheer fright they hurry off at once to the station.

THE JOURNEY UPRIVER

Finally the boat is repaired, and the time has come to start the two-month voyage from the Central Station to Kurtz's Inner Station, deep in the heart of the jungle. The crew is composed of Marlow, the manager, three or four of the pilgrims, and around 30 cannibals they enlist along the way.

Marlow remembers the weird stillness of the jungle, a stillness that isn't anything like peacefulness. Conrad continues his personification of the wilderness: "It looked at you with a vengeful aspect." It makes Marlow think of the prehistoric jungle, and it seems monstrous, bewitching, creepy—and patient, as if it were waiting to devour them. The river is treacherous, too; there are snags and shallows everywhere.

The Africans on board are cannibals, but instead of eating each other they've brought along a load of hippo meat that eventually goes rotten and starts to stink. Marlow is especially fascinated—and disturbed—by the tribal villages they pass. As the Africans catch sight of the boat, they break into an "incomprehensible frenzy" of greeting. They're so different from the Europeans Marlow knows it's hard to believe they're the same species. And yet "They howled and leaped, and spun, and made horrid faces; but what thrilled you was just the thought of their humanity like yours—the thought of your remote kinship with this remote and passionate uproar." Marlow is faintly terrified to feel a responsive chord stirring within himself. He knows there's something in these savage rites that attracts him, that has meaning to him.

When he asks his audience, "You wonder I didn't go ashore for a howl and a dance?" he isn't only joking. And he isn't only joking, either, when he tells them the reason he didn't: "I had no time." Work, we've already learned, is one of Marlow's highest values. Now work saves him from losing his mind in the jungle. When you have to attend to guiding a boat and looking out for snags, and chopping wood for the steam engine to burn, you don't have time to think about "the inner reality" of that primitive call. You stay busy with the "surface-truth" of doing your job, instead of brooding and driving yourself crazy.

But the possibility remains: the lure of savagery could take *somebody* in. We're going to see that happen eventually.

As if Marlow didn't have enough to keep him busy, he also has to keep an eye on his African fireman. (The fireman watches over the steam engine, making sure that the boiler doesn't run out of water to make steam with.) He has a few months of training and he knows how to watch the boiler, but he no more understands what he's doing than a dressed-up dog understands why he's wearing clothes. "What he knew," Marlow tells us, "was this—that should the water in that transparent thing disappear, the evil spirit inside the boiler would get angry through the greatness of his thirst, and take a terrible vengeance." At the same time the fireman is working with modern technology, he's standing there with his teeth filed and his hair shaved into patterns and a bone through his lip. When Marlow calls him "an improved specimen," he's being sarcastic, and he's also showing a certain pessimism toward the civilizing ideals—the notion of carrying light into the darkness—that everybody in Africa was mouthing at the time. These people were trying to justify their being in Africa by demonstrating how much progress they'd brought the Africans. But in this case, as with the torch in Kurtz's painting, enlightenment doesn't seem to have banished the darkness. How much good has his smattering of education done Marlow's fireman?

THE MESSAGE. THE FOG. CANNIBALS

Fifty miles from the Inner Station the boat steams up to an old hut with a pile of wood in front and a faded message scrawled on a piece of board: "Wood for you. Hurry up. Approach cautiously." The manager figures it must have been left by that "miserable trader," the non-Company man he'd told his uncle he would like to hang. Marlow also finds a battered old book on seamanship, with notes in the margin that appear to be written in code ("cipher"). But why bring a book about ocean sailing out into the middle of nowhere, and why go to the trouble to make notes in code? "It was an extravagant mystery."

The next evening they stop about eight miles below the Station. Marlow is eager to press on and meet Kurtz at last, but they've been warned to approach cautiously and sailing up in the dark would be rash. They drop anchor in the middle of the river.

When the sun rises they find themselves in the middle of a thick fog "more blinding than the night."

NOTE: In this instance Conrad reverses the usual associations of light and dark: here whiteness is threatening. This isn't the only point where such a reversal occurs. There's also the "whited sepulchre" of Brussels, for example. And in general it's the white race in Africa, not the black one, that's darkly evil.

Around eight or nine o'clock the silent fog is pierced by a loud, despairing cry. It stops, and then a horrible tumult of voices rises up from the banks. The terrified pilgrims dart into their cabins to grab their rifles.

The blacks on board, who are in unfamiliar country themselves, have a different reaction. They seem interested and attentive—but not frightened. Marlow talks to their young leader (a figure of far more dignity than any of the ridiculous pilgrims), who tells him, "Catch 'im. Give 'im to us." Rather amused, Marlow asks what they would do with their captives. "Eat 'im!" the young cannibal curtly replies, and turns away.

Marlow isn't as shocked as you might expect, because it suddenly dawns on him how hungry these men must be. The whites eat mainly out of tin cans they brought with them; but the hippo meat that the blacks brought along was thrown overboard by the pilgrims, who couldn't stand the rotten smell any longer. Now the poor blacks have nothing to eat. They're paid three pieces of brass wire weekly, which they're supposed to trade for food with villagers along the way. But most of the villages have turned out to be either abandoned or unfriendly, or else the unsympathetic manager, who has plenty of canned food of his own, hasn't wanted to stop the boat.

In fact, now that he thinks about it, it amazes Marlow that these 30 cannibals who must be practically starving haven't made a meal of the five white men on board. After all, what's to stop them? Starvation, Marlow knows, is the most horrible hardship you can face. But something restrains these men from gobbling up their taskmasters. "Restraint! What possible restraint?" Yet there it is, a tremendous mystery.

NOTE: Restraint is as important a value to Marlow (and to Conrad) as work is. If people didn't exercise self-control, society would turn into a jungle. There's a special irony operating here, since these typical inhabitants of the jungle are showing such amazing and unexpected restraint. The irony will deepen later, when we encounter a highly "civilized" white man of whom you would expect restraint, who's shown no restraint at all.

Meanwhile, the obnoxious pilgrims are quarreling about which bank the cries came from. The manager halfheartedly urges Marlow to risk setting sail in the fog, but Marlow refuses. The river is too treacherous, it's hard enough to keep from sinking the boat when he can see the river; blinded by the fog, it would be impossible. Besides, Marlow doesn't really think they're going to be attacked. For one thing, any warriors who tried coming out in a canoe would get lost in the fog. But what really convinces him they're probably safe is the way the cries sounded. They didn't seem threatening, Marlow says; "they had given me an irresistible impression of sorrow," as if the sight of the steamboat had filled these people with "unrestrained grief." Marlow, as it turns out, will be proved half-right: right about the grief, but wrong about the attack.

THE ATTACK

The fog finally lifts, and the boat sets off again. Pay particular attention to Conrad's technique in the episode that follows. Conrad has often been called an "impressionist" novelist, and it's easy to see why from his description of the attack. Marlow gives us a string of unconnected impressions, telling us not what happened but exactly what he saw and felt. Only afterward does he put his impressions together and make sense out of them. We get a series of sensations followed by a deduction: Marlow is annoyed to see his poleman (the man who operates the pole with which they test the depth of the water) lie down flat on the deck, and is amazed when his fireman sits down in front of the furnace and ducks his head. Just then he catches sight of a snag ahead of them. At the same time, he notices a shower of sticks whizzing around him. Finally he puts it all together and makes the deduction: "Arrows, by Jove! We were being shot at!" Notice, by the way, that in his series of impressions he includes the sighting of the snag, which doesn't relate to the arrows and the actions of the poleman and the fireman, but which has equal rank as a sensation.

They get around the snag, barely, and Marlow dashes into the pilot-house (which contains the steering wheel) to close the shutter on the land side. The black helmsman (the man who operates the steering wheel) is hysterical, stamping and snorting and steering so badly that they're only ten feet from the bank. Marlow has to lean all the way out to grab the shutter, and when he does, all at once he makes out the whole swarm of naked arms and legs and chests, the army of tribesmen.

Marlow spots another snag ahead, but before he can get a good look at it, the pilgrims on deck below start firing wildly, and he's blinded by the smoke rising from their rifles. The Africans on shore start to howl, and the blacks on the boat raise a warlike whoop in return. A rifle explodes at Marlow's back— the fool of a helmsman has abandoned the wheel, thrown open the shutter Marlow just closed, and he's firing the rifle at the bank. Marlow makes a dash for the wheel. Since he can't see the snag, the best he can do is steer close to the bank, where he knows the water is deep, and hope for the best.

In the incident that follows we again get an excellent example of Conrad's impressionist technique. The crazy helmsman is still at the open shutter, shaking the empty rifle and yelling at the shore. Suddenly he drops the gun overboard and falls against the steering wheel. He appears to be holding a long cane at his side; it looks like in wrenching it away from one of the warriors on shore he lost his balance and fell back. Somehow they clear the second snag. Then Marlow feels something warm and wet on his feet, and looks down. At once he puts his impressions together and realizes what's happened. His feet are covered with blood: the helmsman was speared and he's bleeding to death on the floor of the cabin. Marlow reaches for the line of the steam whistle and sends out a series of screeches. The warlike yells stop, and the attackers let out a long wail of fear and despair before they flee in terror.

One of the pilgrims appears in the doorway, and Marlow puts the horrified man at the wheel. Actually, the uppermost thought in his mind is to get out of his bloody shoes and socks. It isn't unusual for people in extreme situations to fasten their minds on such details, and Marlow's fixation on his shoes is comic and gruesome at the same time. But we may also wonder whether irritation and hardship aren't taking their toll on Marlow's nerves. The doctor in Brussels had warned him to "avoid irritation" and dropped hints about madness (I, 2). Is Marlow, perhaps, getting closer to the brink of insanity?

"He is dead," the pilgrim observes from the steering wheel; and Marlow agrees rather inanely, "No doubt about it," adding that by this time Mr. Kurtz is probably dead, too—murdered by these hostile natives.

KURTZ

At this point Marlow breaks off his tale and launches into a long, rambling discussion of Mr. Kurtz—who hasn't yet appeared on the scene. This would be an odd technique for most novels. But for a story being told aloud it seems absolutely right: nowhere do we get a stronger sense of Marlow's speaking voice.

When Marlow says, after the attack, that Kurtz is probably dead by now, it suddenly occurs to him how badly he had wanted to talk to him. He's heard all about Kurtz's gift of expression; he wanted to hear him himself, and now that he's lost the chance he's almost on the verge of tears. Marlow admits that part of the reason he was so upset was that he'd become a little unbalanced. For one thing, he'd had several small fevers while he'd been in the jungle. And, as he points out, his nerves were in such a state that he'd just thrown a pair of perfectly good shoes overboard.

But as it turned out, Marlow tells his listeners bitterly, he did get a chance to hear Kurtz talk—and he heard more than enough. He alludes to a girl, and he tells them he finally put Kurtz's ghost to rest with a lie. But then he's startled at his own words. "Girl! What? Did I mention a girl? Oh, she is out of it—completely." He repeats his convictions about the beautiful illusions of women, and how men "must help them to stay in that beautiful world of their own." Then he says something about "the disinterred body of Mr. Kurtz saying, 'My Intended.'"

NOTE: By now you'll probably be thoroughly confused. Conrad is playing with our curiosity by dropping hints about what will happen later in the story. Did Kurtz die, we wonder. Did his corpse really talk about his "Intended"? Is that the girl Marlow is talking about?

Marlow now divulges the truth about Kurtz. The wilderness, he tells his listeners, had made Kurtz its own. He was unable to resist; you can't possibly imagine what solitude, "utter solitude without a policeman," can do to a person's mind. The only people who are safe from that kind of madness are the fool, who's too stupid to realize that he's "being assaulted by the powers of darkness," and the saint, "deaf and blind to anything but heavenly sights and sounds." (You'll see examples of both in the pages to come.) But the only protection that the rest of us have—Marlow repeats his favorite nostrum—is work, "your power of devotion, not to yourself, but to an obscure, backbreaking business."

Kurtz represents words, not work; Marlow imagines him simply as a voice. He fell prey to the jungle; his nerves went wrong. He participated in "inconceivable ceremonies" and "unspeakable rites." The "powers of darkness claimed him for their own," and he took "a high seat among the devils of the land."

NOTE: Critics have disagreed about Marlow's vagueness here. Some feel that Conrad owes us a fuller description of Kurtz's crimes, and that by being indefinite he was dodging the issue. Others think that these obscure suggestions are much eerier than any explicit description could be. (Once again we should call to mind Conrad's statement that explicitness "is fatal to the glamour of all artistic work, robbing it of all suggestiveness.") Of course, today we're inclined to want all the scandalous details that a Victorian audience preferred to leave unmentioned.

Instead of getting more explicit, Marlow tells a disturbing story about a high-flown report Kurtz wrote for an organization with a high-flown name, the International Society for the Suppression of Savage Customs. The report began by observing that the white man with his superior technology (weapons, for example) seemed like a god to the primitive African (a rather ominous observation, Marlow adds, in light of what later happened). Its subject was the amazing power to do good that the white man had. But scrawled at the bottom of the last page, much later, was this chilling note: "Exterminate all the brutes!"

Marlow says, with bitter sarcasm, the Kurtz's report demonstrated "the unbounded power of eloquence—of words—of burning noble words." It went on and on about doing good, but there were no practical suggestions about how to do it. What Marlow respects is work, not words. Whenever anybody starts spouting high ideals he gets suspicious, because experience has taught him that ideals are too often just a mask to hide ugly intentions. The best example is the trading companies who are always talking about helping and guiding the Africans when what they're really doing is putting them in chains. In a sense, that terrible scrawled sentence is the one lightning-flash of truth that breaks through the cloud cover of the white man's lies; it's the evil secret of the white man.

The saddest irony is that Kurtz actually believed in the ideals everybody else was just repeating mechanically. The man with the most elevated beliefs turns out to be the one who sinks the lowest. But at least he isn't one of the fools who don't even perceive that the darkness is calling them. "Whatever he was," Marlow tells his listeners, "he was not common." Keep this statement in mind. It sets Kurtz up as the opposite of the characterless manager, lacking in all extraordinary qualities, whom Marlow described as nothing more than a "common trader" (I, 4).

But saying he wasn't common is the most Marlow can say for Kurtz. He doesn't think getting to him was worth the death of his helmsman—a preference for a black life over a (degraded) white one that would certainly shock his racist colleagues.

THE INNER STATION

The mention of the black helmsman returns Marlow's thoughts to the thread of his story. He already missed his dead helmsman terribly, he tells us. True, the man wasn't much of a sailor, but they'd been working together for months, and over that time a subtle bond had formed—a bond Marlow recognizes, admittedly, only once it's broken. And he feels "a claim of distant kinship" with him. Marlow has already told us about the "remote kinship" he felt with the savages he saw on the voyage upriver (II, 2). But that was more abstract, and it was also negative— it made him wonder about the savage buried somewhere in himself. But he misses the helmsman as you would miss a colleague or a friend; he recognizes his humanity. "Poor fool!. . . . He had no restraint, no restraint—just like Kurtz." It wouldn't be such an extraordinary reaction if it weren't so isolated, set off by the racist brutality of the other whites.

The pilgrims and the manager are gathered out on the deck when Marlow drags the body out of the cabin and tips it overboard. They're rather piously shocked to see him dump the remains so promptly, but he has a good reason. He's heard an ominous murmur from the cannibals below, and as much as he sympathizes with their hunger, Marlow the Victorian doesn't sympathize by any means with savage practices: "I had made up my mind that if my late helmsman was to be eaten, the fishes alone should have him." He's also anxious to take the steering wheel from the hands of the inept pilgrim behind it.

As Marlow steers, the pilgrims chatter (another instance of work versus words). They figure (wrongly) that Kurtz is dead and the station burned to a cinder by hostile Africans. And they proudly congratulate themselves for having slaughtered so many of them. But Marlow saw them aiming high and shooting wildly. He maintains (rightly) that the Africans fled in terror at the sound of his whistle.

The boat is still headed for the Inner Station, or whatever is left of it, but the manager prudently wants to get as far back downriver as they can before dark. But even as he's speaking they steam up to a clearing, and they behold the Inner Station—decaying, but in one piece. It has no fence, but Marlow spots what must be the remains of one—six upright posts with what look like ornamental carved balls on top (remember these).

An odd figure is shouting and beckoning them eagerly from the bank: young, beardless, blue eyed, and with so many brightly colored patches neatly sewn all over his clothes that he reminds Marlow of a harlequin, the traditional Italian clown who dresses in motley. His face, like a clown's face, is constantly changing from merriment to gloom and back again. He directs the manager and the pilgrims uphill toward Kurtz, and stays behind himself, jabbering to Marlow. Marlow is uneasy about the Africans in the bush behind the station, but the harlequin assures him there's nothing to worry about: "They are simple people." He even goes so far as to claim they "meant no harm" by the attack, though when Marlow stares at him, speechless, he's compelled to add, lamely, "Not exactly." Nevertheless, he advises Marlow to keep enough steam on the boiler to operate the steam whistle, which frightens them far more than rifles (so Marlow was right).

Something the harlequin says suggests that he's making up for a long silence. "Don't you talk with Mr. Kurtz?" Marlow asks him, and he immediately becomes reverent: "You don't talk with that man—you listen to him." Marlow learns that the young man is a Russian who ran away from school and became a sailor, first in the Russian, then the English navy. "When one is young," the harlequin tells him, "one must see things, gather experience, ideas; enlarge the mind." Two years ago he had set out for the interior of the jungle with "no more idea of what would happen to him than a baby." The hut downriver where they found the pile of wood and the message is his old house.

Marlow returns the book he found there. "You made note in Russian?" he asks, solving the mystery of the "coded" notes. When he tries to find out why the natives attacked, the Russian grows shamefaced: "They don't want him to go." (Not an hour before everyone was assuming Kurtz had been killed by hostile Africans.) Now Marlow has the solution to two mysteries—the coded notes, and also the enigmatic cry of despair that came from the Africans when they spotted the steamboat approaching.

CHAPTER III

THE RUSSIAN'S STORY

As the excitable, clownish young Russian prattles on, Marlow envies his pure "spirit of adventure," not to mention "the glamour of youth" in him. But he doesn't envy him his devotion to Kurtz. We already know how little value Marlow places on talk. Now the impressionable youth tells him how Kurtz's eloquence swayed him and made him into a follower.

In his digression on Kurtz (II, 5), Marlow had cited the saint and the fool as types of people who, even alone in the jungle, were safe from the lure of madness, the call of the darkness: "Of course you may be too much of a fool to go wrong—too dull even to know you are being assaulted by the powers of darkness." The Russian is just such a character; dressed in motley, he even looks like a conventional fool. He's a simple man utterly lacking in malice, he couldn't harm a fly. Even though he's lived side-by-side with a man who's sunk to the most gruesome depths of evil, he seems untouched by the horror of it; he hardly even recognizes it. There's something sweet and likable about him, though you certainly can't approve of his attachment to Kurtz. He explains it simply: "I have no great thoughts"; and Kurtz, we know, is made up of one "great thought" after another—which isn't to say that the thoughts have any more substance than the empty, high-toned words of his report to the International Society for the Suppression of Savage Customs. But the simple, trusting fool can't make this distinction.

The station house is decayed. It turns out that Kurtz hardly lived there. He would disappear for long stretches into the forest, where he'd discovered a lake and gotten to know the Africans living around it. His guns made him seem like a god to them. Remember the words of Kurtz's report to the International Society: the white men "must necessarily appear to them [savages] in the nature of supernatural beings—we approach them with might as of a deity" (II, 5). Kurtz had used these Africans as his personal army to raid others for ivory. He isn't a brilliant trader after all, just another ruthless plunderer, no better than the "burglars" of the Eldorado Exploring Expedition. Once he even threatened to shoot the Russian, who was hording a small quantity of ivory—"because he could do so, and had a fancy for it, and there was nothing on earth to prevent him from killing whom he jolly well pleased." Nothing, that is, but the restraint he lacks. The law of the jungle, as it's expressed here in the words of Kurtz, recalls the words of the manager's despicable uncle: "Get him hanged! Why not? Anything—anything can be done in this country." Kurtz isn't, ultimately, a much better man.

Kurtz hated what was happening to him, the Russian continues, but the wilderness had a grip on him and he couldn't tear himself away. Marlow, meanwhile, is nervously sweeping his telescope along the side span of the jungle. He spots an object so startling that he reels back in surprise. Earlier he had mentioned the ornamental balls on the upright posts in front of the house; through the telescope he sees that these carved balls are really human heads.

Returning to a favorite theme, Marlow reflects that the heads showed that Kurtz "lacked restraint in the gratification of his various lusts." He also thinks Kurtz ultimately understood this failing: "I think the knowledge came to him at last—only at the very last." (This is a foreshadowing that you should keep in mind; later on it will provide a clue to the meaning of Kurtz's final, enigmatic words.) But when the young Russian ventures to tell Marlow more about the dark ceremonies Kurtz took part in, Marlow cuts him off angrily (disappointing curious readers, perhaps). Suddenly he's too disgusted to hear more details; he feels as though he's been confronted by a horror far worse than "pure, uncomplicated savagery," which he says "has a right to exist—obviously—in the sunshine."

NOTE: Savages may be primitive, but they aren't evil. Whatever Conrad means by the darkness, it isn't, finally, simple savagery. Savages may be immersed in the darkness of ignorance (the darkness that "enlightenment" is supposed to combat), but not in the darkness of evil—Kurtz's darkness. That wicked aspect of the darkness enters the picture only when somebody civilized plunges to savagery—it's the darkness of atavism. It isn't a disgrace to be uncivilized, unless you were civilized to begin with.

Marlow is disgusted with the Russian, too, who has disgraced himself at least in the sense that he's "crawled as much as the veriest savage of them all" in bowing down to the "magnificent eloquence" of Kurtz. But circumstances are too much for this poor, loyal fool, and he breaks down: he's been struggling to save Kurtz's life, he hasn't slept for ten nights, there's been no medicine, no proper food, Kurtz was "shamefully abandoned . . . . Shamefully! Shamefully!" We know from Marlow's earlier hint that the manager sabotaged the steamboat, that he may be right.

KURTZ. HIS MISTRESS. DEPARTURE OF THE RUSSIAN

A group now appears from behind the house, and more than two thirds of the way through the novel Kurtz finally makes his appearance, borne on a stretcher. Suddenly a cry pierces the quiet afternoon (as a cry had pierced the silence of the fog that morning) and the clearing fills with an army of barbarous warriors. Unless Kurtz says the right thing to them now, the Russian whispers, they'll all be slaughtered. Marlow bitterly resents being at the mercy of a villain like Kurtz. He can see him out there, emaciated, phantomlike; and he can hear his strong, deep voice. Of course, it's appropriate that Kurtz, the man of words, turns out to be a booming voice and not much more. Apparently he says the right thing, because the savages vanish into the forest and Kurtz is carried onto the boat. He's still heavily armed with the weapons that made him a god to the Africans.

NOTE: The prototype for Kurtz was Georges Antoine Klein, a French employee of a Belgian concern in Africa, who died of dysentery, much like Kurtz, aboard a steamer on the Congo River. (Conrad was aboard the steamer when Klein died.) Dysentery is an emaciating disease, and its horrifying effects are probably behind Marlow's description of his first view of Kurtz: "I could see the cage of his ribs all astir, the bones of his arms waving. It was as though an animated image of death carved out of old ivory had been shaking its hand . . . . "

The mention of ivory is important symbolically. Earlier, during his digression on Kurtz, Marlow said, "The wilderness had patted him on the head, and, behold, it was like a ball—an ivory ball" (II, 5). Now his whole body looks like ivory. This is a fitting image, since Kurtz has been possessed by the greed for ivory, just as the ruthless Spanish conquistadors were possessed by greed for the gold of Eldorado. This isn't the only image for his obsessive greed. Marlow tells us, "I saw him open his mouth wide—it gave him a weirdly voracious aspect, as though he had wanted to swallow all the air, all the earth, all the men before him."

As the warriors move about indistinctly in the forest, Marlow turns his gaze to a magnificent African woman striding back and forth along the shore, her ornaments flashing in the dying sunlight. Wild-eyed, passionate, dangerous, she symbolizes to Marlow the very soul of the jungle—savage, a thing to admire but also to fear. Note that his phrasing specifically connects her with the wilderness. Earlier he had sensed in the jungle "an implacable force brooding over an inscrutable intention" (II, 2); now he tells us the woman had "an air of brooding over an inscrutable purpose." She comes up to the steamer and gazes fiercely at the men on board; then, at a signal from her, the warriors dart out of the forest, ready for blood. Everyone waits tensely. But now that she's shown her power, she turns away and walks slowly into the forest.

The opposition between Kurtz and the manager comes to a head. Marlow hears Kurtz in his cabin ranting furiously, "You with your little peddling notions—you are interfering with me." The manager emerges, trying to look compassionate but obviously gleeful at the downfall of his rival. Immediately he expresses his disapproval of Kurtz's crimes: "Deplorable! Upon the whole, the trade will suffer." Kurtz was entirely right about his "little peddling notions": it isn't Kurtz's evil or his brutality that disturbs the manager; it's his bad business sense. In fact, the worst he can say for Kurtz's "vigorous action" is that "the time was not ripe" for it—as if it ever would be. But bureaucrat that he is, the manager can hardly wait to deliver the final blow by filing a full report with the Company.

Marlow is disgusted. "it seemed to me I had never breathed an atmosphere so vile, and I turned mentally to Kurtz for relief—positively for relief." Kurtz may be evil, but something about the manager is even worse; if the two of them represent "a choice of nightmares," then Marlow is ready to choose. Just as he was prepared to lie to the brickmaker in order to help Kurtz, whom he hadn't even met, he's prepared to defend him—even though he's learned the ugly truth—before the manager. Why does he prefer the nightmare of Kurtz? We should recall his statement that "Whatever he was, he was not common" (II, 5); in fact, he tells the manager, Kurtz is "a remarkable man." The manager isn't remarkable or even competent (we've already seen the chaos of his Central Station); he's merely a "common trader" (I, 4), but also petty and conniving and greedy and, in his own colorless way, just as murderous and evil, under the surface of appearances, as Kurtz, though there's no speck of greatness in him as there is in Kurtz. Conrad uses him to stand for the crimes of all the white men in Africa—hence the depth of Marlow's disgust. Marlow gets rid of him with a sarcastic remark.

Presently the Russian interrupts his grim thoughts. He's afraid Marlow is going to repeat what he's learned about Kurtz from him once he gets back to civilization. Marlow assures him that Mr. Kurtz's reputation is safe with him. (He doesn't know, as the end of the book will reveal, how truly he speaks. Marlow has made his choice of nightmares, and now he's destined to stay loyal to Kurtz.) The Russian is also nervous about his own life, and Marlow, remembering the conversation between the manager and his uncle, tells him he's right to be: "The manager thinks you ought to be hanged." The man of patches decides he'd better clear out at once. But first he makes a final admission to Marlow: Kurtz himself ordered the attack on the steamer, thinking it would scare the party away or that they'd give him up for dead—which they almost did. "He hated sometimes the idea of being taken away." And then he vanishes in the night.

NOTE: Another set of images you should take note of is part of a pattern that's been developing since Chapter I. Marlow describes Kurtz as a "phantom," an "apparition," a "shadow." Back when he was first sailing to Africa on the French steamer, Marlow got an odd feeling that something was keeping him "away from the truth of things, within the toil of a mournful and senseless delusion" (I, 3). At the Central Station, the air of plotting, the philanthropic pretense, the pilgrims' talk and their phony show of work were "unreal"—"By Jove! I've never seen anything so unreal in all my life" (II, 5). And when he let the brickmaker think that he really did have influence in Europe, he told us, "I became in an instant as much of a pretence as the rest of the bewitched pilgrims" (II, 5).

The "phantom" Kurtz belongs to the realm of illusions, the realm of words. He's even deluded himself: "I'll carry my ideals out yet—I will return. I'll show you what can be done," he cries to the manager. To this unreal world Marlow opposes (as we already know) the value of work, which gives you the chance to find "your own reality" (I, 6). To take one example, the Russian's little book on seamanship, with its charts and numbers and diagrams, had "an honest concern for the right way of going to work," and thus it struck Marlow as "something unmistakably real" (II, 3).

Marlow makes an exception in his principles for women, who don't work and who live in a world of "beautiful illusions" of which he seems to approve. We'll hear more about this subject in the final pages of the novel. It's hard to say why he should excuse women—except that for a Victorian writer like Conrad women simply didn't work, that was the order of things. (We may disagree strongly today.) In any case, women's world of "beautiful illusions" is very different from the ugly realm of delusions that Kurtz has created in the jungle.

KURTZ'S ESCAPE. DEPARTURE

That night Marlow wakes up remembering the young Russian's vague warning: "I don't want any harm to come to these whites here. . ." On an impulse he gets up to have a look around. The fires of Kurtz's army are flickering in the forest, and Marlow can hear the regular beat of their drum and an occasional burst of yells. When he goes to check Kurtz's cabin, he finds him missing.

At once Marlow feels overpowered by a "pure abstract terror" far beyond any fear for his own skin. Obviously the presence of Kurtz has taken on a deep meaning for him. But he also knows that the boat is in deadly danger. If Kurtz reaches the camp of the warriors, he could order them to attack. Marlow takes off after him without waking anybody else—he wants to deal with Kurtz alone. In fact, he tells us that he was "jealous of sharing with any one the peculiar blackness of that experience."

Why has Kurtz's presence become so important to Marlow, and why does he feel that he has to deal with Kurtz all by himself? Partly because in the fight he's about to put up for Kurtz's soul, he'll be looking deep within his own. Marlow's voyage into the heart of the jungle has also been a voyage into the heart of darkness within himself, a journey into the dark depths of his own personality. All the way upriver, Marlow has been aware of the call of the darkness, just as he's been aware of the beating of the drums. The manager and the pilgrims are like the fool Marlow said is "too dull even to know" the powers of darkness are assaulting him (II, 5). But Kurtz, like Marlow, heard the call, and it overpowered him. Clearly Marlow sees a little bit of himself in Kurtz, and it frightens him.

There's an air of madness in his pursuit. Marlow has been growing increasingly unstable. His mind wanders to various unrelated images, and as he circles around to cut off Kurtz's escape route, he's even giggling to himself. He hears the monotonous beat of the African drum and confuses it with his own heartbeat. Some readers regard this moment as the climax of Marlow's inner journey, the moment when he perceives that the darkness is not outside him, but inside. But unlike Kurtz, Marlow has the restraint to resist its call, even when the call is coming from within himself.

They are about 30 yards from the nearest fire. Kurtz is crawling on all fours like an animal toward a witch-doctor, wearing the horns of an animal—an image that sums up his reversion to beastlike savagery. When Kurtz hears Marlow coming, he stands up, still seemingly unreal—"pale, indistinct, like a vapor."

But his voice is as usual real and strong, and if he shouts it could be all over for Marlow.

Kurtz's attempt to get back to the tribe, Marlow tells us, isn't a conscious choice but an instinctual one. The wilderness has him under its spell, and something inside him—"the awakening of forgotten and brutal instincts, the memory of gratified and monstrous passions"—is pulling him back. But while his instinct is drawing him back, Marlow tries to appeal to his other side, his intellect. "Believe me or not, his intelligence was perfectly clear—concentrated, it is true, upon himself with horrible intensity, yet clear; and therein was my only chance." He has to figure out a way to lure Kurtz back to the boat, and he hits on the idea of stroking his vanity, his desire for fame and glory, the "horrible intensity" of his egoism. As Kurtz mutters about his "immense plans," the "great things" he was going to accomplish, Marlow tells him he'll be "utterly lost" if he doesn't return, but that if he does, "Your success in Europe is assured."

"And I wasn't arguing with a lunatic, either," Marlow says, verifying the Russian's earlier claim that Kurtz couldn't be mad. But he also knows that beyond his sane intelligence Kurtz has another side: "his soul was mad. Being alone in the wilderness, it had looked within itself, and, by heavens! I tell you, it had gone mad." And his soul is what's drawing him irresistibly back to the darkness. But though he has "a soul that knew no restraint," he understands—intellectually—the horror of what's happened to him. Remember the Russian's explanation: "He hated all this, and somehow he couldn't get away." Now, when Marlow makes his appeal to Kurtz's intellect, Kurtz has what he needs to triumph over his brute instincts, his mad soul—the "warning voice of a kind neighbour . . . whispering of public opinion," as Marlow had put it earlier (II, 5). He wants to overcome himself, and so he listens. And he returns to the boat.

Clearly Marlow's exhaustion is more than physical. It isn't just Kurtz's soul he's been grappling with, but his own as well. But once again his tasks as skipper intervene to keep him from looking too deeply into himself. The boat leaves, with Kurtz aboard, at noon the next day. (The struggle had taken place near the opposite hour, midnight. Appropriately, the contest for Kurtz's soul happens in the heart of the night, the heart of darkness; and Marlow, having won, leaves with Kurtz in the heart of the day.) The African army has gathered ominously on the banks of the river. When Marlow asks Kurtz if he understands their wild cries, he replies with a mysterious smile—"Do I not?"—intimating that it isn't just the language he understands, but the savagery as well.

Marlow pulls the string of the steam whistle to frighten the warriors away. The Africans flee in terror, with the exception of Kurtz's savage mistress, who "did not so much as flinch, and stretched tragically her bare arms after us over the sombre and glittering river." (Remember this image; it will recur at the end of the novel.)

KURTZ'S DEATH

As the boat steams swiftly downstream, Kurtz's life is ebbing away. Marlow has the grim double duty of overseeing his dilapidated steamboat and of watching Kurtz die. The trip is especially unpleasant as the loathsome manager is watching the demise of his rival with obvious satisfaction.

As Kurtz's body fades to nothing, his voice remains strong to the last. He doesn't stop talking until he's dead. But his subject matter disappoints Marlow after all the talk he's heard about Kurtz's ideas. Mostly he talks about his dreams of fame and fortune, many of which are "contemptibly childish." His fantasies of wealth and fame don't seem so different from those of the pilgrims or the explorers of the Eldorado Expedition. He doesn't say much that would identify him with the "gang of virtue," though he often repeats the kind of newspaper platitudes Marlow heard in Brussels from his aunt. This is fitting, too, since as it turns out Kurtz was a journalist: "He had been writing for the papers and meant to do so again." (What better occupation could there be for the man of words?) But when the boat breaks down, Marlow has to spend most of his time making repairs instead of listening to Kurtz (again, work versus words)—"unless I had the shakes too bad to stand." Whether his shakes come from the onset of a fever or the start of a mental breakdown isn't quite clear, but we do know he's been deeply upset by his encounter with Kurtz.

Kurtz raves on, never fully aware either of the depths to which he sank at the Inner Station or of his approaching death. "His was an impenetrable darkness." One night it becomes so impenetrable that when Marlow brings in a candle he can't see the light.

At once Kurtz knows that he's about to die. A change comes over his face as if a veil had been torn away, and he has a final vision, a "supreme moment of complete knowledge." Although Marlow doesn't know what it is he sees or suddenly understands, he hears his final words: "The horror! The horror!"

Marlow goes out to the mess room for dinner, but the meal is interrupted by the manager's young servant, who announces contemptuously, "Mistah Kurtz—he dead." Considering that only a short time before Kurtz had been adored as a god, the "tone of scathing contempt" is an ironic comment on his ineffectuality, his ultimate weakness. The idealist who dreamed of moving mountains, who "desired to have kings meet him at railway-stations on his return," doesn't even have the respect of the servants.

Marlow stays in the mess room to finish his meal, and as usual his behavior shocks the pilgrims who are always piously keeping up appearances. ("However, I did not eat much," he adds dryly.) Conrad certainly means us to interpret his reason in symbolic terms: "There was a lamp in there—light, don't you know— and outside it was so beastly, beastly dark." A lamp may not be much to hold against the universal dark, but it's something.

NOTE: What is the meaning of Kurtz's final, chilling words? Conrad provides a couple of clues. Marlow says that the heads around the station house "showed that Mr. Kurtz lacked restraint in the gratification of his various lusts," that there was a deficiency, a lack of something, under all his magnificent eloquence; and he adds, "I think the knowledge came to him at last— only at the very last" (III, 1). Now he tells us that with these words Kurtz "had pronounced a judgment upon the adventures of his soul on this earth." It seems clear that at least on one level "the horror" refers to the abominable deeds he committed out there in the jungle. The words are a form of revulsion, of repentance, of final, sorrowful knowledge.

But the way these words continue to haunt Marlow (and have continued to haunt readers of Conrad) may lead us to wonder if they don't carry a larger meaning as well. Though there's an element of madness to Kurtz, he's remained lucid enough for us to wonder whether in casting off all restraints in the jungle, he has faced, or found, some dark truth about the cosmos, a truth that horrifies him. Are his words a pronouncement on the universe we all inhabit?

The 1890s were an era of pessimism in Victorian England. The ideal of progress had dominated the 19th century; it was widely believed that science would eventually create a perfect world. But by the end of the century it was obvious that the Industrial Revolution, far from creating a perfect world, had only created new forms of misery. Technology could lead to enslavement and death—as it had in Africa. Kurtz symbolizes this failure of technology. After all, he goes to Africa with high and beneficent ideals as an "emissary of light" (in the phrase of Marlow's aunt), but the darkness prevails. Kurtz is the hope of the 19th century perverted, the optimism that failed because it failed to acknowledge its own heart of darkness.

Darwin's theory of evolution had also justified a certain optimism. After all, if his theories were correct, then the history of life on our planet was a history of progress. Each form of life was higher than the one it evolved from; there was a constant upward movement. But by the end of the century the Victorians had also recognized the other side of the coin: no matter how high we ascend, we're still bound to the lower forms of life. Marlow says as much when he's feeling the attraction of the savages along the river: "The mind of man is capable of anything—because everything is in it, all the past as well as all the future" (II, 2). Thus the possibility of reversion, of atavism, is always there. Kurtz travels to Africa thinking he's the future, and what he finds in himself out there is the dim, dark past. We can read his final words not only as a judgment of his own life, but as a warning against a condition that threatens us all. "The horror" is what he finds in the darkness, and the darkness, he knows, is something that exists in all of us.

But what exactly is the darkness? In general, we can safely say that the darkness represents the opposite of civilization. Near the beginning of the book Marlow observes, "We live in a flicker—may it last as long as the old earth keeps rolling! But darkness was here yesterday" (I, 1). (Compare the opening of Genesis: "And the earth was without form and void; and darkness was upon the face of the deep.") If the light of civilization is only a flicker, then isn't the darkness more powerful, surrounding us in space as well as in time?

The darkness also represents the unknown. Thus Africa, traditionally the Dark Continent, is "a place of darkness" for Marlow (I, 2). We live on a planet surrounded by darkness, and there is a mysterious darkness deep within ourselves. Marlow's point in telling his tale is that we'd better acknowledge that mysterious part of ourselves and learn to live with it—as he did—or it will sneak up on us and overpower us, as it did Kurtz, whose darkness becomes "impenetrable."

But you shouldn't confuse the darkness with simple savagery, which, as Marlow says, is something that has "a right to exist—obviously—in the sunshine" (III, 1). After all, even brute savagery represents a stage in the development of civilization. Marlow even has a grudging admiration, or at least sympathy, for the savages he meets in Africa—they're certainly no worse than the whites.

In fact, Conrad sometimes reverses the traditional associations of light with good and dark with evil. The darkness of the jungle is certainly threatening. But other images of evil and of the unknown are white, for example, the fog that surrounds the steamboat before it's attacked. The city of Brussels, that capital of hypocrisy, is a "whited sepulchre." Above all, the monstrous villains Marlow encounters on his journey come not from the dark race but almost without exception from the white one.

The "heart of darkness" refers both to the jungle ("The brown current ran swiftly out of the heart of darkness"—III, 4) and also to Kurtz (his eloquence doesn't hide "the barren darkness of his heart" —III, 4), and thus, by extension, to the rest of us.

Although Marlow recognizes the darkness, and although his tone is generally pessimistic, he doesn't succumb to despair. After all (as we'll see in the pages to follow), Marlow survives his ordeal—barely. Unlike Kurtz, he has the ideals of work and restraint to oppose the call of the jungle. These may not seem like much in the face of a universal darkness (just as the lamp in the mess room seems pretty small against the "beastly dark" outside), but modest as they are, they manage to see him through. Conrad was certainly pessimistic when he opposed the encompassing darkness to the glib ideas of Victorian progress, but there's a big difference between pessimism and despair. The darkness exists, Conrad was saying; acknowledge it and oppose it.

MARLOW'S ILLNESS AND RETURN

Following Kurtz's death, Marlow catches a fever that very nearly kills him. (This is partly autobiographical: Conrad came down with dysentery during his voyage on the Congo.) Marlow finds his struggle with death "the most unexciting contest you can imagine," and is distressed that he can find no final pronouncement as strong as Kurtz's. "This is the reason why I affirm that Kurtz was a remarkable man. He had something to say. He said it . . . . He had summed up—he had judged." After all, grim as it is, Kurtz's final whisper represents "the expression of some sort of belief." Without moral beliefs you can't make moral judgments, you can't think something is a horror without a standard of good to compare it to. Obviously Kurtz failed to live up to his own standard, but at least he had one. So he can recognize the evil he performed, unlike the rest of the whites in Africa, who would be shocked if you told them they were doing anything immoral.

Marlow goes back to Brussels, and his words suggest that he's suffered a mental breakdown as well as a fever: "It was not my strength that wanted nursing, it was my imagination that wanted soothing." As Kurtz has entrusted him with a packet of papers, various interested parties show up to lay their claims. The Company sends a representative to retrieve whatever might help in further exploitation of the territory; Marlow informs him, coldly but truthfully, that the papers don't have that sort of value. (Obviously he's satisfied at being able to place himself at last in open opposition to the odious Company.) A cousin of Kurtz's claims some family letters and memoranda. From this man Marlow learns that Kurtz was a fine musician, a fact that conforms with what we know of Kurtz's character—musicians being often sensitive and high strung. Marlow also receives a visit from a journalist colleague of Kurtz's. This man talks admiringly of Kurtz's talents as a speaker; he thinks Kurtz had the makings of a great radical politician. This, too, we can believe: by now we've heard a good deal about Kurtz's humane ideals and about the power he had to sway people with his speech. The journalist's remark that Kurtz "could get himself to believe anything" is a little more ambiguous, though, since it suggests that Kurtz's high ideals may not have gone very deep. Considering how totally he deserted them, this makes sense, too. Marlow gives this man Kurtz's report to the International Society for the Suppression of Savage Customs (having been careful to tear off the scrawled postscript), and the journalist carries this set of platitudes contentedly away.

THE LIE

More than a year after Kurtz's death, Marlow visits his Intended, the woman he was engaged to, bearing a packet of letters and a portrait of her that Kurtz had given him. As he approaches the house, he remembers again Kurtz's final stare, "embracing, condemning, loathing all the universe," and his final words. (This passage suggests that those words go far beyond a mere self-evaluation.)

In the upsetting scene that follows, it keeps getting darker and darker. Literally, of course, this is because of the sunset. But in this scene Marlow's spirits sink lower than anywhere else in the book (he has "something like despair" in his heart), and the gradually encompassing darkness parallels his deepening bewilderment. In Africa he successfully opposed the darkness; now, suddenly, his victory doesn't seem so final.

Mr. Kurtz had participated in "unspeakable rites" and had gone to his grave with "unspeakable secrets" in Africa. But in this quiet drawing room in Brussels, Marlow gets the panicky sensation that he "had blundered into a place of cruel and absurd mysteries not fit for a human being to behold." He thought he had left the darkness in Africa, where you could blame it on the jungle, but he's about to find out that the darkness is universal.

The Intended is as eager to break her silence as the Russian had been: "She talked as thirsty men drink," of Kurtz's goodness and his nobility and, of course, his eloquence. Her belief in Kurtz is a "great and saving illusion that shone with an unearthly glow in the darkness, in the triumphant darkness from which I could not have defended her—from which I could not even defend myself." Marlow has given his opinions previously about the "beautiful illusions" of women, but face-to-face with this awful delusion he can't be so smugly patronizing. In fact, as she goes on heaping praises on Kurtz—"It was impossible to know him and not to admire him," etc.—he begins to despair. Note that the "great and saving illusion" is what Marlow connects with the light shining against the growing darkness: "But with every word the room was growing darker, and only her forehead, smooth and white, remained illumined by the unextinguishable light of belief and love." If this light burns from a mere illusion, is it really "unextinguishable"?

A gesture she makes, stretching her arms against the fading sheen of the window, reminds Marlow of that final tragic gesture of Kurtz's African mistress. While this deluded woman talks on, Marlow keeps remembering the real, the despicable Kurtz, and "The horror! The horror!" keeps echoing in his mind. The portrait of the Intended had revealed a "delicate shade of truthfulness" in her features, but Marlow doesn't test it. When she asks him to repeat Kurtz's last words, he tells her, "The last word he pronounced was—your name."

She cries out in triumph, then collapses weeping. Marlow is thunderstruck at his lie. We know how much he hates a lie (I, 5). We've seen him dodge telling the full truth on certain occasions; we've even seen him let the brickmaker go on believing something that wasn't true. But we haven't seen him lie outright—until now. The truth, he says, "would have been too dark—too dark altogether . . . ."

Is the darkness, then, the ultimate truth, and light not just a flicker but an illusion as well? When do "beautiful illusions" become ugly delusions? Kurtz's "horror" has begun to seem like Marlow's own judgment on the world of lies we live in, and on this anguished note he breaks off his tale.

EPILOGUE

A brief paragraph brings the novel to a close. The Director notices that they've missed the turn of the tide, but now they can proceed.

Marlow's story has had its effect on our narrator, at least. At the outset his senses were full of the light on the Thames, and when he thought of the great British sailors he called them "bearers of a spark from the sacred fire" who had carried light into the unknown reaches of the world. Now his mind is full of darkness. "The offing was barred by a black bank of clouds, and the tranquil waterway leading to the uttermost ends of the earth flowed sombre under an overcast sky—seemed to lead into the heart of an immense darkness."

A STEP BEYOND

Test and Answers

TEST

1. Marlow got his post as a steamboat skipper _____
   A. through his uncle's influence
   B. when his predecessor was killed
   C. upon retirement from the British Navy

2. When the company doctor learned that _____
   Marlow was sailing to the interior, he asked,
   A. "Could you bring me back an elephant's tusk?"
   B. "Do you expect to gain an audience with Mr. Kurtz?"
   C. "Ever any madness in your family?"

3. As a company agent, Kurtz _____
   A. failed to meet his quota repeatedly
   B. sent in more ivory than anyone else
   C. taught the Africans ballroom dancing

4. The brickmaker described Mr. Kurtz as _____
   I. a prodigy
   II. an emissary of pity and science
   III. the devil's partner
   A. I and II only   B. II and III only
   C. I, II, and III

5. On the way up the river, Marlow despaired _____
   of
   A. ever seeing Edinburgh again
   B. ever hearing the eloquence of Kurtz
   C. bringing back enough ivory to make the trip worthwhile

6. Reference is made to Kurtz's report for   ____
  A. The Africa-Asia Society
  B. The International Society for the
    Suppression of Savage Customs
  C. The Stanley-Livingstone Memorial Society

7. Joseph Conrad's remarkable Mr. Kurtz is ____
said to personify
  A. the dark side of every man
  B. grace under pressure
  C. the lamb surrounded by the wolves

8. In a postscript to his report, Kurtz is alleged ____
to have scribbled
  A. "Exterminate all the brutes!"
  B. "Africa for the Africans!"
  C. The horror! the horror!"

9. Kurtz may be viewed as a symbol of   ____
   I. the white man's failure in Africa
   II. the cultural aridity of the dark
    continent
   III. treachery to one's brothers—mankind
  A. I and II only B. I and III only
  C. II and III only

10. Marlow's lie to the woman at the end of the ____
story dealt with Kurtz's
  A. last words
  B. message to the manager
  C. renunciation of his mistress

11. What is the meaning of the title *Heart of Darkness*?

12. Examine Conrad's narrative technique in *Heart of Darkness*.

ANSWERS

1. B **2.** C **3.** B **4.** A **5.** B **6.** B

7. A **8.** A **9.** B **10.** A

11. The "darkness" of the title is the book's most pervasive symbol. In general, it refers to the incomprehensible and the unknowable; more specifically, it refers to that negative force, whatever it is, which stands opposed to the Victorian era's ideals of progress. Marlow finds this brute force in the jungles of the Congo, but he learns that it isn't restricted to the jungle. Certainly it exists where civilization and progress haven't yet penetrated, but it exists in advanced society, too. (Conrad associates images of darkness and gloom with the city of London.) Further, Marlow learns that the darkness exists not just externally, as a force, but also internally: we all carry the capability for reversion, for evil, somewhere within us.

Consequently, the "heart" of the title is a pun. On the one hand, it means "center": the heart of darkness is the center of the jungle, specifically the Inner Station where Kurtz dwells. But it also means "the human heart": Kurtz is black hearted in the traditional sense of the word—cruel, wicked. And since Marlow hints that we all have darkness somewhere in our hearts, then perhaps the "heart of darkness" refers, bleakly, to the human situation: striving toward the light of progress, but pulled back by the power of darkness.

12. In using a narrator who's supposed to be spinning a tale aloud, not writing it down, Conrad imitates the methods of an oral story-teller. And so he adopts a number of techniques that were at the time unusual in a novel. For example, there are sudden jumps in time, flashbacks, as when Marlow, pursuing Kurtz on the riverbank, suddenly recalls the old woman with the cat in Brussels; or flashforwards, as when Marlow, describing the attack on the steamboat, suddenly jumps ahead of himself to tell about Kurtz, who at that point hasn't entered the story yet. There are pauses, hesitations, digressions, and repetitions that seem right for a speaking voice, but would have no place in a "written" work. In his digression on Kurtz (II, 5), Marlow mentions a girl: "even the girl herself—now—"; then he's silent for a long time; and then he begins, "Girl! What? Did I mention a girl?" Such a passage adds to the illusion of a speaking voice.

Conrad's so-called impressionism is an important part of his technique. He often relates a series of impressions before putting them together to decide what they mean. During the attack, Marlow sees the poleman lie flat on deck, then the fireman squat before his furnace, and then a number of little sticks in the air. Only then does he deduce, "Arrows, by Jove! We were being shot at!" (II, 4).

Term Paper Ideas

1. Not only does Marlow survive an ordeal and live to tell the tale, he also thinks his tale needs to be heard. He thus resembles several similar narrators: Lemuel Gulliver of *Gulliver's Travels* by Jonathan Swift; the title character in Samuel Taylor Coleridge's "The Rime of the Ancient Mariner"; Ishmael in Herman Melville's *Moby-Dick*. Compare Marlow to any of these figures, or to a similar narrator.

2. Examine the theme of self-restraint, paying particular attention to the contrast between the manager and Kurtz, and between the cannibals and the pilgrims.

3. The primary narrator says that to Marlow "the meaning of an episode was not inside like a kernel but outside, enveloping the tale which brought it out only as a glow brings out a haze"; and further, "we were fated . . . to hear about one of Marlow's *inconclusive* experiences." How well do these statements describe the story Marlow tells?

4. Kurtz's savage mistress and his Intended are linked by a gesture at the end of the novel. Explain what these two women stand for. Be sure to consider both their positive and their negative aspects.

5. Examine Conrad's use of light/dark and white/black symbolism. Make sure you include instances where he reverses the expected associations, as in the "whited sepulchre" of Brussels and the fog that's "more blinding than the night."

6. Analyze Conrad's use of the frame—the device that places Marlow and his audience before us at the beginning, the end, and (a couple of times) in the midst of the novel. What function does it serve? Disposing of the frame would simplify the novel; do you think it would improve it?

7. "And this also has been one of the dark places of the earth." Before his main tale, Marlow speculates about what it would have been like for a Roman sailing into the wilderness of England 1900 years earlier. Relate this opening monologue to the rest of the novel.

8. Throughout his tale Marlow treats the jungle as if it were another character in his story: "The high stillness confronted these two figures with its ominous patience, waiting for the passing away of a fantastic invasion" (II, 1); "It looked at you with a vengeful aspect" (II, 2). This technique of giving human characteristics to something inhuman is called *personification*. Examine Conrad's personification of the jungle. What effects does he achieve with it?

9. Examine the attitude of the various characters toward Kurtz: the chief accountant, the brickmaker, the manager, the Russian, the Intended. Trace the way Marlow's initial conception of Kurtz changes into ultimate knowledge.

10. Explain why the choice between loyalty to Kurtz or to the manager is "a choice of nightmares" for Marlow, and why he chooses to be loyal to the more obviously evil of the two men.

Glossary

Alienest   Psychiatrist

Assegais   Light, slender spears

Astern   Toward the stern, or rear, of a boat

Boiler   The tank or container in which water is heated into steam to provide power for the steamboat. A *vertical boiler* is a relatively simple type that takes up little space.

Bows (in the bows)   Toward the bow, or front, of a boat

Calipers   An instrument with two curved, movable legs, used to measure the diameter of a thing

Concertina   A kind of small accordion

Drake, Sir Francis   English navigator (1540?–1596). The first Englishman to sail around the world, which he did in his ship the *Golden Hind* (1577–80). Participated in the defeat of the Spanish Armada (1588).

Estuary   The mouth of a river

Fairway   The navigable part of a river

Falernian wine   A well-known ancient wine which was made in southern Italy

Fireman   The man who tends the steamboat's furnace, stoking it with wood

Fleet Street   An important business street in London

Franklin, Sir John   British explorer (1786–1847). With his ships the *Erebus* and the *Terror*, he set out for the Arctic in 1845 to search for the Northwest Passage—an expedition that ended, tragically, in the deaths of all members.

Funnel   Smokestack

Holmsman   The man at the helm (steering mechanism), who steers the boat

Martini-Henry   A kind of military rifle

Mephistopheles   In the Faust legend, the wily devil who tempts Faust

Mizzenmast   A mast toward the back of a boat

Offing   The distant part of the sea visible from the shore

Pilot-house   The enclosed cabin in which the helmsman steers the boat

Ravenna   The site of an important Roman naval base in northern Italy

Scow   A flat-bottomed boat with square ends, used for transporting freight

Sounding-pole   The long pole used to sound, or measure, the depth of the water

Stern-wheel   The paddle wheel at the back (stern) of a steamboat

Stone   14 Pounds (British measurement) 16 stone = 224 pounds

Time contracts   Legal contracts to work for a specified period of time. Such contracts were used to exploit the African natives, who had little understanding of European law.

Trireme   An ancient Roman ship with three tiers of oars on each side

Yawl   A small sailboat

The Secret Sharer

THE STORY

The Plot

A young captain in the British merchant marine has just set out on his first command, starting through the Gulf of Siam (Thailand) and heading home. He was hired unexpectedly only two weeks before. So, while his men know one another well, he's the only stranger on board, and he's nervous about the impression he'll make, especially on his first mate, a fussy and not very bright seaman, and his sneering second mate, who's the only man aboard younger than the captain.

The captain volunteers to take the anchor watch, staying on deck late to watch for the wind they need. While alone there, he's astonished to discover a swimmer clinging to the ship's ladder, and he takes him aboard. The man's name is Leggatt, and he's a fugitive from the *Sephora*, another British ship anchored nearby. Leggatt was the ship's first mate, and during a terrible storm he killed a mutinous sailor. He was being held to await trial on shore. The captain immediately develops a deep sympathy for him, an identification so strong that soon he's calling him "my second self." He agrees to hide him in his stateroom.

The next day a search party arrives from the *Sephora*, headed by the ship's Captain Archbold. Archbold is neither bold nor intelligent, and according to Leggatt he's such a poor leader that he went to pieces during the storm. The captain protects Leggatt, despite Archbold's suspicions.

Hiding Leggatt proves to be a terrible strain. In order to protect him, the captain has to behave so oddly and give so many peculiar orders that the crew—whose opinions he was so worried about in the first place—begin to think he's crazy. For his part, he becomes so involved in the identity of the secret sharer of his cabin that he finds it difficult to function when he's away from him. One day, after almost being discovered by the steward, Leggatt seems to have disappeared. The captain is more distressed at the prospect of losing his double than of having him found out.

Finally they agree on an escape plan. In carrying it out, the captain demonstrates the bold and resolute action that previously he wasn't sure he was capable of. One night, under the pretense that he's hunting for land breezes, he brings the ship dangerously close to shore. Leggatt escapes, but the crew is terrified. In the darkness the captain can't judge the movement of the ship in relation to the water—until a floppy hat he had given Leggatt comes floating by, showing him that the back of the ship is moving too fast. At the last minute he's able to give the order to change direction, and he saves the ship.

The Characters

The Captain-Narrator

The young captain who tells the story is the embodiment of self-doubt. His lack of resoluteness is a serious shortcoming in a ship's commanding officer, and he's aware of it. This may be the reason he grows so quickly attached to Leggatt: Leggatt knows his own mind and is utterly resolute. But in deciding to hide Leggatt, the captain puts himself in a situation that almost drives him over the edge into insanity.

Because he's young and unsure of himself and on his first command and a stranger to the ship, the captain is overly concerned about the opinions of his crew members—he worries so much about what they'll think of him that he almost freezes up. But at the same time he believes firmly in the principle of hierarchy: his word is law, and not to be questioned. When he starts giving senseless and, ultimately, dangerous commands in order to protect Leggatt, he puts his crew to a difficult test: how obedient should you be to a captain who seems determined to sink the ship? The special irony here is that after wanting his crew's good opinion so much, the steps he takes to protect Leggatt make him look like he's going out of his way to lose it.

But though he's not completely admirable, he's a sympathetic figure—partly because the story is told from his point of view. He's far more intelligent than the rest of the crew or Captain Archbold, and as a result he's contemptuous of them in a way that's amusing to read about but would be less amusing if you were a crew member. (Probably we can catch a glimpse here of Conrad the Polish aristocrat surrounded by the boorish sailors of the British merchant marine.)

Nevertheless, in tough situations the captain handles himself, and his ship, like an expert. And he knows how to handle other sailors, too, for example, the rough-mannered Captain Archbold (whom he unnerves with politeness) and the insolent second mate (whom he sharply rebukes). In the final scene, he shows terrific competence by maneuvering his ship out of danger (even though he got it into danger in the first place). It seems clear at the end of the story that he'll make a fine and capable captain.

Leggatt

Unlike the captain, Leggatt is a fully self-possessed young man. He knows his own mind and he knows how to take bold and courageous action—as he does during the storm on the *Sephora*, when he takes matters into his own hands and sets the sail that saves the ship. And he's straightforward about himself: he doesn't try to excuse or soften the impact of his crime (the murder of a mutinous sailor) when he tells the captain about it. (The captain does the excusing for him.) But he has a clear conscience and he's eager to escape. He accepts the captain's help without questioning it or feeling guilty about the nightmare he puts the captain through as a result. He doesn't suffer, as the captain does, from looking at things too deeply.

If anything, Leggatt is *too* impulsive. We can admire the directness with which, during an emergency, he knocked down an insolent sailor who was endangering the lives of the crew. But strangling the man to death is a different matter. Since we see Leggatt only through the captain's eyes, though, it's difficult to get a clear picture of him. We may get a sense that the captain is willing to excuse too much in him, but we can also sympathize with the isolation of this hero-criminal from the rest of his crew, and be moved when he tells the captain how much his understanding has meant to him.

Leggatt's personality is convincingly drawn. But what does Leggatt *mean*? The more than fifty references to doubling, the notion that Leggatt is somehow a part of the captain-narrator's self, have tantalized readers ever since the story was first published. Some readers think that Leggatt is the captain's moral conscience; others, that he represents the unconscious impulses below the surface of the captain's mind. Some argue that he symbolizes the criminal side of the captain, the vicious impulses he has to master and dominate; others insist that he stand for the captain's ideal image of himself. And some exasperated readers have decided that all this symbolism is no more than an intellectual tease. According to them, you should enjoy "The Secret Sharer" as the fine adventure it is, and not worry yourself with digging for hidden meanings. You'll have to decide for yourself what you think Leggatt stands for—or if he stands for anything. Whatever meaning Conrad had in mind, he didn't provide us with enough evidence to produce a firm and final interpretation.

Captain Archbold

Captain Archbold, the commanding officer of the *Sephora* (the ship from which Leggatt escapes), can be summed up by the adjectives "spiritless" and "unintelligent." If we can believe Leggatt's story (and Archbold's own version seems to confirm it), Archbold lost his nerve in the middle of the terrible storm, and it was Leggatt who saved the ship. But because Leggatt killed a man, Archbold is unwilling to give him any credit; he attributes the ship's survival, rather dishonestly, to the hand of God, not Leggatt. He adheres to the letter of the law, not granting that there were unusual circumstances around the crime. He's really more concerned about the embarrassment the crime will cause him than the merits of Leggatt's case. He suspects that the young captain may be hiding Leggatt, but his plodding, stupid nature is no match for the younger man's cleverness; the captain easily gets rid of him (though there's a hint that Archbold knows the captain has made a fool of him). Conrad emphasizes his ridiculous side. Thus, even though the captain-narrator's interview with Archbold is tense, it's also funny, because Conrad makes Archbold the butt of several jokes.

Chief Mate

The chief mate, with his "terrible growth of whisker" and his honest devotion to the ship, might be a lovable character in another context. But seen through the contemptuous eyes of the captain, he's an "imbecile" with "the 'Bless my soul—you don't say so' type of intellect." There's certainly nothing vicious about him, just irritating, but circumstances (the captain's decision to hide Leggatt) turn this simple man into a threat. He behaves badly in the crisis, becoming so unhinged (he raises an arm "to batter his poor devoted head") that the captain has to shake him like a child, but he manages to recover himself before the end. (In certain respects—dull intellect, lack of fortitude in a crisis, whiskers—he resembles Captain Archbold.) If the story were told from a different point of view, the mate's position as chief officer under a captain who appears to have lost his mind would make him a more sympathetic figure.

Second Mate

The captain continually chides the second mate (the officer next in line after captain and chief mate) as a "cub," emphasizing his youth and inexperience; he's the only crew member younger than the captain himself. He's rather sour and unlikable. Early on the captain catches him sneering at the chief mate, and soon he's sneering at the captain as well—unpardonable behavior in a subordinate officer. But he gets a stern dressing-down before the end of the story—an important act of self-assertion for the captain, and a much-needed bit of discipline for the second mate.

Steward

The steward (the officer in charge of provisions, and the one who cleans the captain's stateroom) isn't developed as a character, but his predicament provides some of the funnier moments in the story. The captain keeps giving him incomprehensible and ludicrous commands in order to keep Leggatt well-hidden in his stateroom, until the bewildered man is at the point of despair.

Other Elements

SETTING

The action takes place in the Gulf of Siam (also called the Gulf of Thailand), bordered by the Malay Archipelago on the west and Cochin-China (part of Indochina) on the east; the ship sails out of the Mei-nam River (better known today as the Chao Phraya) that flows by the city of Bangkok at the very north of the gulf. (When Conrad took command of the *Otago* in 1888, he, too, sailed from Bangkok.) The ship sails down the Cochin-China coast, and Leggatt makes his escape to the island of Koh-ring, off the coast of Cambodge (Cambodia or Kampuchea).

The shipboard setting emphasizes the isolation of the crew, as does the description of the gulf, which opens the story; the captain has left his friends behind, and he's the only stranger aboard. It's also noteworthy that so much of the story—in particular, Leggatt's arrival and escape—occurs at night, the time for dreams, the domain of the unconscious. To further the association, both Leggatt and the captain wear sleeping suits.

THEME

"The Secret Sharer" portrays the friendship of two men during a time of strain and crisis. Each is able to offer the other something he needs. The captain offers the escaped killer Leggatt both protection from the men who are pursuing him and, eventually, escape. Leggatt gives the captain something less tangible—a lesson that he badly needs in self-possession, self-reliance, and self-control. In the course of the story, the captain learns, largely from the example of the secret sharer of his cabin and his life, how to be a good leader. In protecting him, he has to stop worrying about the opinions of others and assert himself.

But firmness isn't the only quality in a good leader. He needs to be able to act resolutely, too, to give orders when necessary without terrifying himself over what the consequences might be. Captain Archbold is an example of a leader who can't act in a crisis: during the frightening storm that besets the *Sephora*, he can't make himself give the order to set the sail that's their last hope, because he's afraid of losing it. But the young captain maneuvers his own ship through hair-raising danger along the shallow coast in order to help Leggatt escape. After this crisis, he's clearly in full possession of his abilities.

STYLE

Conrad's style here is clean and direct, much simpler than the digressive, garrulous narrative in *Heart of Darkness*. "The Secret Sharer" is a different kind of story; since it employs a more traditional first-person point of view, Conrad doesn't need to imitate the speaking voice of the narrator. But whatever he loses in complexity he gains in directness: the story is suspenseful and exciting in a way that the dense prose of *Heart of Darkness* wouldn't convey. His impressionist method is still in evidence. And when the author pauses for a picturesque description, for example, of the Gulf of Siam and the "swarm of stars" above it in the opening pages of the story, the effects are rich and lovely.

POINT OF VIEW

Imagine what it would be like to have the story narrated by the chief mate, or by Captain Archbold: our sympathy for both the young captain and Leggatt would vanish. A different point of view would create a very different story. If the story had an omniscient narrator who could see into the minds of the various characters, we would lose the fascination of what we *don't* know—Leggatt's motivation. (Is he, essentially, innocent or guilty? Has the captain acted foolishly or wisely in protecting him? There's evidence on both sides.) Finally, imagine the story from Leggatt's point of view. How would he see the young captain—as a true friend, or as a dupe?

The captain bears a certain resemblance to the young Conrad, who sailed his first command under similar windless conditions in the Gulf of Siam (though apparently without stowaways). But unlike Marlow in *Heart of Darkness,* the captain is such a fallible narrator, that is, so untrustworthy in much of what he perceives, that we can't assume he's a stand-in for the author. And, unlike Marlow, he relates events without thinking deeply about them. Marlow is always ruminating, judging, trying to find the meaning in his own tale; the captain-narrator tells his story as if he were unaware that it had any meaning at all. He doesn't guide us in interpreting his tale, and Conrad has kept himself so distant that it isn't clear what he thinks of the events, either. So interpretation rests, even more fully than in *Heart of Darkness,* with you the reader.

FORM AND STRUCTURE

Like the style, the form of the tale is simple and straightforward. There isn't the experimentation, the jumping around in time and space, that you find in many of Conrad's other works (including *Heart of Darkness*). The action all takes place on one ship (except for the brief section in which Leggatt tells his story), and it moves from beginning to end without flashbacks or flashforwards.

In structure, there's a forward movement from ignorance to knowledge—in this case, the captain's self-knowledge. (In this respect, the structure resembles the structure of *Heart of Darkness*.) The young captain is a different and better man—or at least, a better leader—at the end of the story than he was at the beginning. However we ultimately judge Leggatt, it seems clear that the captain has profited by knowing and aiding him.

The Story

Conrad divided "The Secret Sharer" into two chapters. To make discussion easier, the chapters can be subdivided as follows:

CHAPTER I

1. The New Command.
2. Leggatt's Arrival.
3. The Next Morning.

CHAPTER II

1. Captain Archbold of the *Sephora*.
2. Scares.
3. Escape.

Be sure to note that these subdivisions aren't Conrad's. They are used here in order to make the story easier to analyze and discuss.

CHAPTER I

THE NEW COMMAND

"The Secret Sharer" opens with a description of the Gulf of Siam from the deck of a ship—a description that serves two purposes. The exotic locale (Gulf of Siam, Meinam River, Paknam pagoda) would have appealed to the landlocked magazine audience for whom "The Secret Sharer" was specifically written (Conrad meant the story to have popular appeal). But the strangeness of the surroundings also tells us something about the narrator's mental state; he finds the setting in some way "incomprehensible" and "crazy of aspect," and completely lacking (for the moment) in signs of life. The narrator is a young captain in the British merchant marine, and this is his first command; he feels not only the disquiet of unfamiliar surroundings, he also feels literally alone—alone against the rest of the ship. He was appointed unexpectedly only two weeks before, and he doesn't know either the men or the ship. But the men all know each other and the ship quite well. So this first description reflects the uneasiness of an isolated outsider. Just before the sun goes down, he spots the masts of a neighboring ship and realizes he isn't entirely alone. He doesn't know it yet, but this ship will set the plot in motion and make his first command more harrowing than he ever feared.

At dinner we're introduced to the two chief officers below the captain. The first mate is an older man, bearded and fussy and not unduly intelligent. (Later the narrator will call him an "imbecile.") He's always saying witless things like "Bless my soul! You don't say so!" and trying to account to himself for the most trivial incidents, such as how a scorpion got into his inkwell. (He'll soon be trying to account to himself for something less trivial, the captain's seeming craziness.) The young captain obviously thinks he's a stupid bore, but he also wants his respect and his approval because he's new.

The second mate is the only person aboard who's younger than the captain. He's a rather sour young man with a tendency to sneer, a quality highly inappropriate to a subordinate officer, and one that the captain immediately disapproves of. The second mate informs them that the ship the captain spotted is another English ship, named the *Sephora*.

Throughout the meal, the captain-narrator stresses the alienation he felt as a stranger on board. Obviously he has very little self-confidence. After dinner, as a gesture of good will to the weary crew, he tells the first mate that he'll take over the anchor watch himself, that is, he'll stay awake on deck, watching for the wind they need to start their journey. It's an unusual offer because the watch usually goes to those lower in the ship's hierarchy. The young captain immediately regrets his offer, which he'd made to win the approval of the sailors. As we'll see, the captain is morbidly alert to the reactions of his crew; and soon enough he'll be giving them reason to wonder if he isn't really crazy.

Once everyone is asleep and he's alone on deck, he begins to feel more peaceful. True, he's isolated as he was in the opening passage, but he's so nervous about the opinions of the crew that being alone is a relief. He begins to look foward to the voyage home. After all, he reflects, he's a good sailor; "the sea was not likely to keep any special surprises expressly for my discomfiture." The reflection is ironic, since even as he's thinking, the sea is holding a surprise—a swimmer who will turn his whole life upsidedown. But right now he's rejoicing in the nautical life and in "the great security of the sea as compared with the unrest of the land," a life with "no disquieting problems, invested with an elementary moral beauty" of straightforwardness and singleness of purpose. Again, the observation is heavily ironic, for the young captain is about to face a situation far less straightforward, and far more insecure, than anything he's faced on land.

NOTE: As with *Heart of Darkness*, "The Secret Sharer" has an autobiographical element. In 1888 (more than twenty years before he wrote the story), Conrad took over command of the *Otago*, sailing out of the Meinam River into the Gulf of Siam—precisely where the ship in "The Secret Sharer" is sailing. He, too, was a new captain on his first command aboard a ship that already had a crew. He must have been nervous and insecure; such feelings plagued Conrad throughout his life. As in the story, the journey through the gulf was made especially difficult because there was so little wind.

The first mate is also based, at least in part, on the first mate of the *Otago*, who was suspicious of the young Polish captain (partly because he had hoped for the command himself). Conrad later recalled: "His eternally watchful demeanour, his jerky, nervous talk, even his, as it were, determined silences, seemed to imply—and, I believe, did imply—that to his mind the ship was never safe in my hands . . . . On our first leaving port . . . a bit of manoeuvring of mine amongst the islands of the Gulf of Siam had given him an unforgettable scare." As we'll see, this is exactly what takes place during the final pages of the story.

LEGGATT'S ARRIVAL

As the captain is moving placidly around the deck, he notices that the ship's rope ladder has been left hanging over the side. At first he's annoyed, but then instead of blaming the sailors he blames himself for breaking their routine. Thus we get an idea of his compassion for his crew and his strictness toward himself. Again he regrets seeming eccentric by having taken the anchor watch.

But as he goes to haul the ladder in, he's astonished to see a man clinging to the bottom of it. His first reaction is a "horrid, frost-bound sensation" of pure terror—he sees no head. Once again, he overreacts because of his own nervousness, in his words, "my own troubled incertitude."

The man on the ladder exhibits the very opposite qualities. Although "hesitating" and "slightly anxious" at first (we'll find out in a moment why he has good reason to be), he becomes "calm and resolute" as soon as he finds out he's talking to the ship's captain, and he asks to come on board. His "self-possession" not only impresses the captain-narrator; it also makes him feel calm and resolute himself. And almost everything Leggatt says gives evidence of his "strong soul." (For example, he tells the captain he wasn't sure whether to come aboard or to keep swimming until he sank from exhaustion; and the captain recognizes his sincerity.) So from the very first moments of his meeting with Leggatt, the captain finds qualities in him that he desperately needs but feels that he lacks.

There's another reason the captain so readily accepts him. Leggatt is, like himself, a stranger aboard the ship, the only other stranger, in fact. They have the bond of mutual isolation. The captain has come to regard the crew as his judges, but he doesn't have to prove himself to Leggatt. So his company is a relief, and immediately a "mysterious communication" is established between them.

The captain takes the naked man up on deck, outfits him in one of his own sleeping suits, and hears the story of his crime. Leggatt was the first mate of the *Sephora*, whose captain was an irresolute, nervous man, not a decisive leader. (In this respect, perhaps he wasn't so different from the captain Leggatt is speaking to.) During a violent storm it had become necessary to set the only sail they had left. It was the ship's last hope, but the captain couldn't work up the courage to give the order and Leggatt had to take over himself. While they were struggling to set the sail, he was faced with the insolent behavior of the crew's worst member: "He wouldn't do his duty and wouldn't let anybody else do theirs." They were in a life-or-death situation, and finally the exasperated

Leggatt turned around and struck him. They started to fight, but as they were fighting, a huge wave crashed over the ship. The worst of the storm lasted for ten minutes, and when it cleared somewhat, the crew found Leggatt with his hands on the neck of the insolent sailor, who was dead from strangulation.

From the way Leggatt depicts his crime, we get a picture of him as a man of direct, instinctual action. He takes over the setting of the sail himself, and when the sailor creates trouble, Leggatt "turned round and felled him like an ox." He tells the captain straightforwardly, "I've killed a man," without trying to soften the impact of the crime (though you can sympathize with a first mate who hits a mutinous sailor). "It's clear that I meant business," he says, "because I was holding him by the throat still when they picked us up. He was black in the face. . . . They had rather a job to separate us, I've been told." These aren't the words of a man who's trying to make excuses for himself.

The captain takes Leggatt down to his own stateroom, and now a pattern of references on the "double" theme begins. It will continue unabated for the rest of the story—for instance, "my double," "the secret sharer of my life." The two men are the same size, both quite young (Leggatt is even younger than the captain), and they're both graduates of the training ship *Conway* (where Leggatt, not surprisingly, won a prize for swimming). Even Leggatt's name has a double pair of double letters.

NOTE: Once their "mysterious communication" has begun, it becomes terrifically important for the captain to continue identifying with Leggatt. But why? One reason, certainly, is that Leggatt has the qualities of resoluteness and self-confidence that he lacks. But Conrad makes so much of the theme of the double that its significance comes to seem deeper than simply that.

Leggatt goes on with the story of his imprisonment and escape. For the trembling captain of the *Sephora* he has nothing but disdain: "Devil only knows what the skipper wasn't afraid of (all his nerve went to pieces altogether in that hellish spell of bad weather we had)." (We'll meet the skipper of the *Sephora* in the next chapter, so we'll be able to judge whether this description is likely.) He felt essentially innocent— under the circumstances, but not in the eyes of the law. The captain wouldn't agree to let him escape, but he seized the opportunity when it presented itself, and swam that very evening from the *Sephora* to the young captain's ship. He's certain that a search party from the *Sephora* will show up tomorrow.

As Leggatt talks, the captain-narrator again expresses his self-doubt and his admiration for Leggatt when he imagines Leggatt planning out an escape: "a stubborn if not steadfast operation; something of which I should have been perfectly incapable." Though Leggatt isn't expecting the circumstances that allow him to escape (the steward accidentally leaves his door unlocked after delivering dinner), once he has the idea he's in the water without a second thought, swimming as hard as he can even though he doesn't know where. Only later does he spot the captain's ship. The ladder hanging overboard is just a lucky accident (and it won't be the last one in the story).

We also see that Leggatt is a man with a capacity for violence, a man who certainly could commit a murder. He twice says that he didn't want to make an imperfect escape because if the crew had come after him, "somebody would have got killed for certain"; he admits he would have fought off anybody who laid a hand on him, "like a wild beast." But the captain pays little attention to this side of his character. He's immediately convinced (almost before hearing the story) that Leggatt acted justifiably, if not legally, and he's willing to endanger his own position in order to protect him.

Just as the captain's attraction to Leggatt is understandable, so is Leggatt's to the captain: he's provided him with an almost miraculous escape. But it's more than that. Leggatt says that his imprisonment aboard the *Sephora* was "a confounded lonely time"; and when the captain had spotted him in the water, he says, rather than being frightened, "I—I liked it." Leggatt is even more isolated from his shipmates than the captain feels from his own. Though one is an outlaw and the other a stranger, both feel threatened by their own communities; they feel an immediate kinship.

It's quite late by now, and Leggatt is exhausted. The captain puts him to bed and he falls asleep at once.

NOTE: Leggatt's tale is based on an actual event, though not one that Conrad was involved in; he knew of it through hearsay and newspaper accounts (it was widely reported). In 1880, the chief mate of the *Cutty Sark* got into an argument with one of the seamen, who threatened the mate with a heavy bar. The mate wrested the bar from the seaman and knocked him unconscious with it; three days later the seaman died. The mate escaped (with the help of the skipper), but he was eventually captured, tried, and sentenced to seven years for manslaughter.

Leggatt, of course, is a flesh-and-blood character in the story; but there are indications that Conrad regarded him as a representative, in some sense, of part of the narrator's consciousness. (He considered naming the story "The Secret Self," "The Second Self," or "The Other Self.") For example, Leggatt shows up at night, he appears to rise from the depths of the sea, and he wears the captain's sleeping suit—all symbols associated with dreams and the unconscious. And it's abundantly clear, from the more than 50 references that link the two of them, that Conrad was fascinated (he seems almost obsessed) with the theme. But what, then, does Leggatt represent? There have been almost as many answers to that question as there have been readers of the story. Some readers think that Leggatt represents the captain's better side, his ideal self; others are sure that he stands for the criminally impulsive side of himself that the captain has to master. And some readers think that as a symbol Leggatt has been overinterpreted; they argue that the story should be enjoyed as a fine adventure but not much beyond that. Ultimately, you'll have to decide for yourself what Leggatt is supposed to mean (or what he means to you). Conrad constructed a tantalizing puzzle, but he neglected to give us the key.

THE NEXT MORNING

Having put Leggatt to bed, the captain feels too nervous to go to sleep himself. (He's the only character without the peace of mind to sleep. It was on account of his insomnia that he volunteered to take the anchor watch in the first place.) He sits on the couch, exhausted and bothered by a knocking in his head—which turns out to be the steward knocking on his stateroom door the next morning. He's slept after all.

This passage gives us a fine example of Conrad's impressionist method, though in staying true to the captain-narrator's impressions it cheats a little bit. "I was not sleepy; I could not have gone to sleep," the captain reports; and we don't have any reason not to believe him. (He believes himself.) So when in what seems like the next moment he's disturbed by a knocking in his head that turns out to be the steward knocking on the door, and we suddenly realize that several hours have passed, we're as surprised as he is (or was). We feel as if we're experiencing the sensation (of knocking), and then the deduction (it's the steward: several hours have passed) at the same moment he does.

At this point, the comedy of the steward begins; it will continue, increasingly silly and funny and nerve-racking, through much of the story. The steward is just trying to do his job, bring the captain his morning cup of coffee. So when the captain shouts, "This way! I am here, steward," as if he were miles away, the steward is understandably mystified. He doesn't know that Leggatt is concealed behind the bed-curtains or that the captain fears he'll discover him. He doesn't realize he presents a threat. He knows only what his senses tell him—that the man is behaving bizarrely. The captain behaves just as bizarrely when he returns to warn him to close his porthole (the men above are washing decks): "I jumped up from the couch so quickly that he gave a start." And when he tells the steward that the porthole is already closed, that fact must seem even stranger, since it's "as hot as an oven" in the cabin. A vicious circle has begun. The captain is already more paranoid than he should be about the opinions of his crew members. But now, in order to conceal Leggatt, he's about to begin acting in ways that will really make them wonder about his sanity. And as they start to wonder, he feels doubly insecure.

In fact, when he marches up on deck he spies the steward and the first and second mates gossiping together. They part so hastily when they see him coming that he has no doubt it's his behavior they're talking about. (For a change, his paranoia is justified.) But instead of letting his anxiety make him even more indecisive, he gathers his resolve (perhaps Leggatt is already exerting a healthy effect on him) and barks out "the first particular order I had given on board that ship; and I stayed on deck to see it executed, too." He can't let his crew get the upper hand—that could end up in their discovering Leggatt. He has no choice but to pull himself together and act like the decisive commander he should have been in the first place. That way, nobody will have the nerve to question his behavior, even when it seems erratic. His strategem apparently works. But meanwhile, firm as he is on the outside, he's quaking on the inside. The sensation of having a second self down in his stateroom "distracted me almost to the point of insanity. . . . It was very much like being mad."

NOTE: The references to madness and to breakdown, which continue throughout the story, are particularly interesting: not very long after he wrote "The Secret Sharer," Conrad was to suffer a nervous breakdown.

Leggatt is sleeping so soundly (again, he's associated with sleep and dreams) that the captain has to "shake him for a solid minute" before he wakes up. Then he moves "as noiseless as a ghost" (again, a hint—but only a hint—that there's something less than physical about the double) into the bathroom while the steward cleans the stateroom. Leggatt is very much a night creature; the captain observes his face "looking very sunken in daylight." After the steward's departure, the captain continues on his course of action to keep himself and Leggatt safe. With Leggatt still in the bathroom, he invites the meddling first mate in for some unimportant small talk; "my object was to give him an opportunity for a good look in my cabin" and thus to allay any suspicions the man might have formed about what's going on in there. (At this point, though, there isn't much reason for him to have formed any.) After that, captain and double remain behind closed doors until the announcement that a ship's boat (the search party from the *Sephora*) is on its way. Leggatt gives a start (one of his few shows of anxiety), and the captain strides up on deck to meet the boat.

NOTE: At this point the first chapter ends. As with *Heart of Darkness*, chapter divisions have less to do with structure than with the fact that the work ran as a serial, in this case in two issues of the American *Harper's Magazine*, August and September 1910.

CHAPTER II

CAPTAIN ARCHBOLD OF THE *SEPHORA*

The captain of the *Sephora* turns out to be a thoroughly unimpressive man. His stature is "middling," he looks around "vaguely," he's "spiritless" and "unintelligent" and "densely distressed," and we're told that he looked "muddled" and that he "mumbled" in a "reluctant and doleful" way. He makes such a dull impression that our captain-narrator pays him the final insult: he's not even sure Archbold was his name. Of course, he's biased against him from the start. He continues his course of wily action, now pretending to be deaf so that the mumbling Archbold has to raise his voice—and so that Leggatt can overhear everything.

Conrad plays the scene for both tension and comedy. Archbold's plain manners and plodding stupidity make an easy target for the clever and well-educated young captain. For example, the narrator is telling us about Archbold's description of Leggatt's strangled victim: "And as I gazed at him certainly not prepared for anything original on his part, he advanced his head close to mine and thrust his tongue out at me so suddenly that I couldn't help starting back." Such ludicrous moments are even funnier against the background of nerve-racking tension.

Having taken the law into his own hands in protecting Leggatt, our captain sneers at Archbold's stubborn adherence to the letter of the law. When he mentions the setting of the sail (Leggatt claimed he saved the ship by setting their last sail during the storm), Archbold replies piously, "God's own hand in it"—he's readier to ascribe their success to Providence than to a murderer. But something he says rings true with Leggatt's version of the story: "I don't mind telling you that I hardly dared give the order. It seemed impossible that we could touch anything without losing it, and then our last hope would have been gone." (Later Leggatt will insist that Archbold really did fail to give the order, no matter how he remembers it now.) And our captain observes that Archbold is still terrified by the memory of the gale. It was precisely this terror which so disgusted Leggatt.

According to Archbold, he disliked Leggatt from the start. "He looked very smart, very gentlemanly, and all that. But do you know—I never liked him, somehow. I am a plain man." In response, the young captain smiles "urbanely," when urbanity is exactly what Archbold is criticizing. Still identifying with his double, he's as offended as if Archbold were condemning him. And in one sense he is: the plain seafarer attacking the manners of an aristocrat could be pointing a finger at either one of them—or at Conrad, the Polish aristocrat who sailed with common sailors. They must have resented his polite manners as deeply as he disdained their rough ones. And in fact the strategem the young captain chooses for making Archbold uncomfortable is politeness, which the unsophisticated Archbold views as "a strange and unnatural phenomenon."

Little by little, Archbold grows suspicious, but he's intimidated by the icy politeness of his host. He begins to ask leading questions, but the captain refuses to acknowledge his hints. When Archbold begins eying the various doors—Leggatt might be behind any one of them—the captain pretends to think he's interested in the ship. Then he gets even ("I had been too frightened not to feel vengeful") by leading him on a tedious and irrelevant tour. He speaks loudly in order to give Leggatt plenty of warning as they're coming to his own stateroom, and it works: "My intelligent double had vanished." (In the captain's eyes, Leggatt is the only other "intelligent" character. Archbold is specifically "unintelligent"; the first mate is "that imbecile.")

The first mate corners him after Archbold has left. Is he getting more suspicious? The captain manages to put him off, but he knows that the *Sephora*'s men have told his crew about Leggatt's escape.

Exhausted from his deception, the captain drifts toward despair. He and Leggatt can hardly even whisper together. "The Sunday quietness of the ship was against us; the stillness of the air and water around her was against us; the elements, the men were against us—everything was against us in our secret partnership; time itself—for this could not go on forever." Here we get the first hint that they're going to have to plan Leggatt's escape from the ship. And we feel again the threat that makes the two men feel closer than ever.

In the same bleak mood, the captain reflects: "And as to the chapter of accidents which counts for so much in the book of success, I could only hope that it was closed. For what favorable accident could be expected?" Once again, his hopelessness is unflattering in a man whose position calls for him to be resolute. When Leggatt jumped over the rail of the *Sephora*, he didn't expect another ship to be anchored nearby, and he certainly didn't expect its ladder to be hanging over the side. Lucky accidents have gotten him where he is. And a lucky accident will come to the aid of the captain, though in this mood he wouldn't believe it.

From the captain's talk with Archbold, it's apparent that Leggatt's version of events was essentially true. Still, the captain is even more eager to excuse Leggatt's crime than Leggatt is to excuse himself. (He wants to escape, but he isn't protesting his innocence.) The captain places the blame on impersonal forces: "It was all very simple. The same strung-up force which had given twenty-four men a chance, at least, for their lives, had, in a sort of recoil, crushed an unworthy mutinous existence." That's a comforting way of putting it, because it leaves out the damning detail of Leggatt's hands locked around his victim's neck.

SCARES

At last the wind they've been waiting for starts up and the captain takes command of his ship. But he senses that he isn't doing his best job—partly because he's left half of himself down in his stateroom. This missing half might be his unconscious self, or the direct, instinctual side of himself: "A certain order should spring on to [a seaman's] lips without thinking; a certain sign should get itself made, so to speak, without reflection. But all unconscious alertness had abandoned me. I felt that I was appearing an irresolute commander. . . ."

The captain is so lacking in self-possession that when he thinks Leggatt is about to be discovered (to take one example), "I could not govern my voice and conceal my agitation." Leggatt, on the other hand, is "perfectly self-controlled, more than calm—almost invulnerable"; he's "unyielding" and filled with "unalterable purpose." The captain is succumbing to the strain of the situation: "I think I had come creeping quietly as near insanity as any man who has not actually gone over the border." But not Leggatt: "Whoever was being driven distracted, it was not he. He was sane."

The comedy of the steward now gets even broader. The captain has come to hate the sight of him simply because he's in charge of tidying his stateroom. The steward, for his part, is something like a persecuted stooge in a slapstick movie. "It was this maddening course of being shouted at, checked without rhyme or reason, arbitrarily chased out of my cabin, suddenly called into it, sent flying out of his pantry on incomprehensible errands, that accounted for the growing wretchedness of his expression."

One day, for example, as the officers are dining, the captain sees the steward carrying his coat, which has been drying on deck, toward his stateroom. He starts shouting at the man, to alert Leggatt that somebody's approaching so he can slip into the bathroom. The other officers look at him like he's a lunatic. Then he hears the steward opening the bathroom door, and he goes stony from fright. The steward has decided to hang the coat there because it's not quite dry yet. But luckily he just opens the door, reaches in, and hangs it on a hook, so he doesn't see Leggatt squatting in the tub. It's another fortunate accident (and not the last).

The captain's reaction here has two interesting aspects. First, we get another hint—they're never more than hints—that there's something unearthly about Leggatt. When the captain sees him again, "an irresistible doubt of his bodily existence flitted through my mind. Can it be, I asked myself, that he is not visible to other eyes than mine? It was like being haunted." This is a tantalizing suggestion, but it doesn't lead anywhere conclusive, because we know (from Archbold) that Leggatt is real.

NOTE: Conrad may have been playing homage here to *The Turn of the Screw* by Henry James, a novelist he admired to the point of considering him his mentor. In that story, it's never clear whether the ghosts are real, or imagined by the woman who sees them. In the case of "The Secret Sharer," the suggestion acts as another hint that Leggatt on some level represents part of the captain's mind, perhaps his unconscious self.

The other noteworthy aspect of the captain's reaction is his attachment to Leggatt. Only at first is he relieved when the steward doesn't discover him: " 'Saved,' I thought. 'But, no! Lost! Gone! He was gone!' " He's almost as distressed at having lost his second self as at having him found out. And when Leggatt mentions that they need to start planning his escape, his first response is to resist: "Maroon you! We are not living in a boy's adventure tale." But Leggatt argues, logically, that it's even more dangerous for him to stay on board: on a three-month passage he would certainly be discovered. The captain knows he's right, and with shame he perceives that his resistance was "a sort of cowardice." He's going to have to learn to function without the example of Leggatt's self-possession and self-control.

Their reward is their mutual understanding. "It's a great satisfaction to have got somebody to understand," Leggatt assures him. They set the escape for the next night.

ESCAPE

The captain's plan is simple: bring the ship close to shore (on the rather flimsy excuse that he's searching for "land breezes") so that at an opportune moment Leggatt can slip into the water. The two of them study the Cochin-China (Indochina) coast and decide to aim for the large island of Koh-ring, off Cambodge (Cambodia). The only difficulty lies in getting the men to obey the absurd and even dangerous orders that the plan calls for. But the captain gathers his resolve and, with more self-possession than ever before, plays the role of stern commander to the hilt. When the sneering second mate questions the order to open the quarter-deck ports (the outlets at the end of the quarter-deck giving onto the water), he gets the sharp comeuppance he's been needing. The first mate, too, is puzzled and then alarmed. (As we know, there may be an autobiographical element here.)

Our last views of Leggatt are ambiguous. The captain finds him sitting quietly in his stateroom "like something against nature, inhuman." Does this mean that Leggatt really does represent the darker, criminal side of the captain's nature? It's also uncertain whether Leggatt is being sincere when he (at first) refuses the money the captain presses on him. (His main reason for refusing seems to be that he doesn't have a safe place to put it; when the captain offers a handkerchief to tie it in, he doesn't need much more convincing.)

With another ridiculous order, the captain gets the steward out of the way so that he can sneak Leggatt into the sail locker (where the sails are kept). From here he'll be able to steal across the quarter-deck, out the quarter-deck ports, and into the sea. As an afterthought, the captain gives him his floppy hat to protect him from the sun when he reaches land.

With Leggatt hidden in the sail locker, the next order of business is to approach the island of Kohring. The captain sails dangerously close to the shore. Leggatt, we know, is a good swimmer; does the captain need to endanger his ship and his crew to the extent that he does? Is his behavior absurdly dangerous? Or is he using the occasion to assert himself, to show that he's in full control? He demonstrates his nerve, he never lets on that he's frightened, and he certainly manages to scare the daylights out of his crew. The first mate, in particular, goes completely to pieces, much in the manner we heard Captain Archbold had done. The captain has to shake him like a child to make him pull himself together.

The last section of the story is hair-raising to read. In

the shadow of Koh-ring, it's as dark as "the very gate of Erebus," the pitch-dark entrance to Hades. Not knowing the ship well, the captain can't tell whether or which way it's moving in the water. He needs a marker, but there's no time to find something he can drop into the water to judge the position of the ship in relation to the surface. A final lucky accident saves him: the hat he had given Leggatt comes floating by; it must have fallen off when Leggatt went in. From its motion he can tell that their rear is moving too much, and just in time he gives the order to change direction. They barely make it, and the men let out a cheer.

The captain created the danger, but he also rescued the ship. On another level, the captain's irresoluteness brought on a situation that was bad for the ship, and his new ability to assert himself remedies the situation. The hat is a visible symbol of the action he's taken, action he needed to take from the very beginning.

Rather than missing his double, the captain is relieved to have him gone. He makes it clear that from here on out his journey will be a smooth one, "the perfect communion of a seaman with his first command." He hardly thought of his double (he tells us explicitly) during the crisis; at last he feels whole, integrated, and capable in himself. He devotes a few moments to thoughts of Leggatt—"a free man, a proud swimmer striking out for a new destiny." This may strike you as an overly romanticized way to describe a man who, we've just been told, will be "hidden forever from all friendly faces," "a fugitive and a vagabond on the earth." (The man who provided the inspiration for Leggatt was captured and sentenced to seven years.) But the words make a lot more sense if you apply them to the double's double—the captain himself.

A STEP BEYOND

Test and Answers

TEST

1. An immediate problem which the narrator-captain perceived was that   _____
   A. as a newcomer he is unfamiliar with his officers
   B. his ship was barely adequate for the voyage
   C. the surliness of the crew was blatant

2. From his first meeting with Leggatt, the captain   _____
   A. identified closely with the intruder
   B. vowed to protect him
   C. was convinced that he knew the stowaway

3. Leggatt admitted to having murdered his shipmate   _____
   A. in a fit of revenge
   B. in a fight during a storm
   C. to prevent a mutiny

4. The secret sharer had been   _____
   A. a steward on the *Liverpool*
   B. the first mate on the *Sephora*
   C. the bo's'n on the *Mosholu*

5. Stewed chicken, oysters, and sardines were part of   _____
   A. the ship's strange cargo
   B. the stowaway's diet
   C. the captain's dream of his homecoming dinner

6. The peculiar shape of the captain's cabin   _____
   A. made it inevitable that the stranger would be discovered
   B. was altered to conceal Leggatt
   C. allowed him to hide his passenger from the crew

7. At one point, the captain wondered whether   _____
   A. his passenger was merely a figment of his own imagination
   B. his impulsive decision would lead to criminal charges
   C. his passenger's presence would invite disaster for the ship

8. The captain's erratic orders led the crew to believe that   _____
   A. he was hiding his wife
   B. he was an escaped convict
   C. his seamanship was suspect

9. The captain's hat   _____
   A. added to his imposing mien
   B. helped to guide the ship to safety
   C. shielded the stranger's face from the crew

10. Conrad ended his story by describing the stranger as   _____
    A. "my double, my brother, my mirror image"
    B. "the sharer of a sacred mutuality"
    C. "a free man, a proud swimmer striking out for a new destiny"

11. Discuss the theme of courage in crisis in "The Secret Sharer."

ANSWERS

1. A   **2.** A   **3.** B   **4.** B   **5.** B   **6.** C

7. A   **8.** C   **9.** B   **10.** C

11. Two shipboard crises occur in the story—one we witness, the other we hear about—and in both cases there's a man whose courage fails him and a man whose courage pulls the ship through to safety. When the *Sephora* is beset by a storm, its captain, Archbold, loses his nerve and can't act; he's unable to give the order to set the sail that is the ship's last hope, and his loss of nerve endangers the whole crew. Fortunately, his chief mate, Leggatt, takes matters into his own hands and sets the sail, and it's through his courageous and determined action that the ship survives the storm.

We get a parallel situation at the end of the story. The young captain keeps a cool head during the tense moments when his ship is so close to shore that it's in danger of running aground. He's frightened himself—so frightened that he has to shut his eyes rather than watch the shore loom closer—but he never lets his men see his fear, and he never lets fear paralyze him as it paralyzed Captain Archbold. In contrast, the devoted chief mate loses control of his emotions and begins to despair aloud, in front of the crew. His behavior proves that he doesn't have what it takes to be a captain, a leader.

We may surmise that Leggatt provides an inspiration to the initially self-doubting young captain. The captain has the stuff of leadership within him from the start, but his contact with Leggatt nourishes that quality and brings it out.

Term Paper Ideas

1. Why does the captain protect Leggatt, and why does he bring the ship so close to shore that he nearly runs it aground? Write an essay about the morality, or immorality, of his actions. Your view of Leggatt's character will probably affect your view of the captain's conduct.

2. Examine the many references to the theme of the double in "The Secret Sharer." They're impossible to miss—but what, finally, do they mean?

3. Both the captain and Leggatt feel isolated from their shipboard communities. Examine the theme of isolation in the story.

4. Contrast the differing attitudes of Leggatt, the captain-narrator, and Archbold toward Leggatt's actions on the *Sephora* during the storm.

5. "The Secret Sharer" is often nerve-rackingly funny; it's even been compared to a Marx Brothers movie. Examine the comic elements.

Nautical Glossary

Alee Leeward; the direction toward which the wind is blowing. **Hard alee!** All the way leeward

Anchor watch The part of the crew, usually one man, who stays on duty at night while the ship is at anchor

Bare poles Masts without sails

Binnacle The stand on which a ship's compass rests

Break (of the poop) The point where the (poop) deck ends

Coming-to Moving the ship's front toward the wind

Cuddy A small cabin

Deep ship A ship that sits low in the water

Gimbals A device for suspending articles to keep them horizontal despite the motion of the ship

Mainsail haul! An order to adjust the mainsail (on the mainmast) so as to head directly into the wind

Overhaul To slacken (a rope)

Poop (deck) A raised deck at the stern of a ship

Ready about An order used in tacking. To *come about* is to pass from one tack to the other.

Reefed sail A sail whose size has been reduced by folding

Riding light Light shown at night by a ship at anchor

She will weather the ship won't go ashore. **She will never weather** the ship will drift ashore and be grounded.

Shoals Shallows

Square the yards by lifts and braces To set the yards at right angles to the keel and the masts

Stand in To take the ship toward the shore

Stays: in stays Changing to another tack

Sternway Backward motion of a ship

Tack The direction a ship is headed in relation to the position of the sails. To *tack* is to bring the ship into the wind and around to catch the wind from the other side.

Taffrail The rail at the back of a ship

Waist The middle part of the deck

Yard A rod at right angles to a mast, to support a sail

Heart of Darkness
&
"The Secret Sharer"

Further Reading

CRITICAL WORKS

Baines, Jocelyn. *Joseph Conrad: A Critical Biography*. New York: McGraw-Hill, 1960.

Forster, E.M. "Joseph Conrad: A Note," in *Abinger Harvest*. New York: Harcourt Brace, 1936.

Graver, Lawrence. *Conrad's Short Fiction*. Berkeley: University of California Press, 1969.

Guerard, Albert J. *Conrad the Novelist*, Cambridge: Harvard University Press, 1958.

————. "Introduction" to *Heart of Darkness* and "The Secret Sharer." New York: Signet Books, 1950.

Gurko, Leo. *Joseph Conrad: Giant in Exile*. New York: Macmillan, 1962.

Kimbrough, Robert, ed. *Heart of Darkness: An Authoritative Text, Backgrounds and Sources, Essays in Criticism*. New York: W.W. Norton, 1963.

Leavis, F. R. *The Great Tradition: George Eliot, Henry James, Joseph Conrad*. New York: New York University Press, 1963.

Mudrick, Marvin, ed. *Conrad: A Collection of Critical Essays*. Englewood Cliffs, N.J.: Prentice-Hall, 1966. Contains "The Originality of Conrad", by Mudrick; "The 'Unspeakable Rites' in *Heart of Darkness*," by Stephen A. Reid; and "Legate of the Ideal" (pp. 75–82), by Daniel Curley.

Sherry, Norman. *Conrad's Eastern World*. Cambridge: Cambridge University Press, 1966.

———. *Conrad's Western World*. Cambridge: Cambridge University Press, 1971.

Watt, Ian. *Conrad in the Nineteenth Century*. Berkeley: University of California Press, 1979.

Zabel, Morton Dauwen. "Editor's Introduction" to *The Portable Conrad*. New York: Viking Press, 1947.

AUTHOR'S OTHER WORKS

This isn't a complete list, but it includes most of Conrad's major stories and novels with the dates of first publication.

Almayer's Folly, 1895
An Outcast of the Islands, 1896
"An Outpost of Progress," 1897
The Nigger of the "Narcissus," 1897
"Youth," 1898
Lord Jim, 1900
"Amy Foster," 1901
Typhoon, 1902
Nostromo, 1904
The Secret Agent, 1907
Under Western Eyes, 1911
Chance, 1912
Victory, 1915
The Shadow Line, 1916
The Arrow of Gold, 1919
The Rescue, 1919
The Rover, 1923

The Critics

On Conrad's Obscurity

What is so elusive about him is that he is always promising to make some general philosophic statement about the universe, and then refraining with a gruff disclaimer . . . . Is there not also a central obscurity, something noble, heroic, beautiful, inspiring half a dozen great books; but obscure, obscure? These essays [Conrad's *Notes on Life and Letters,* 1921] do suggest that he is misty in the middle as well as at the edges, that the secret casket of his genius contains a vapour rather than a jewel; and that we need not try to write him down philosophically, because there is, in this particular direction, nothing to write. No creed, in fact. Only opinions, and the right to throw them overboard when facts make them look absurd.

—E.M. Forster, *Abinger Harvest,* 1936

On the Meanings of the Darkness

[Marlow's perspective] can be summarised along the following lines: the physical universe began in darkness, and will end in it; the same holds for the world of human history, which is dark in the sense of being obscure, amoral, and without purpose; and so, essentially, is man. Through some fortuitous and inexplicable development, however, men have occasionally been able to bring light to this darkness in the form of civilisation—a structure of behavior and belief which can sometimes keep the darkness at bay. But this containing action is highly precarious, because the operations of darkness are much more active, numerous, and omnipresent, both in society and in the individual, than civilised people usually suppose. They must learn that light is not only a lesser force than darkness in power, magnitude, and duration, but is in some way subordinate to it, or included within it: in short, that the darkness which Marlow discovers in the wilderness, in Kurtz and in himself, is the primary and all-encompassing reality of the universe. . . . In any case, neither Conrad nor Marlow stands for the position that darkness is irresistible; their attitude, rather, is to enjoin us to defend ourselves in full knowledge of the difficulties to which we have been blinded by the illusions of civilisation.

—Ian Watt, *Conrad in the Nineteenth Century*, 1979

On Conrad's Originality, and Where It Falls Short

Conrad's innovation—or, in any case, the fictional technique that he exploited with unprecedented thoroughness—is the double plot: neither allegory (where surface is something teasing, to be got through), nor catch-all symbolism (where every knowing particular signifies some universal or other), but a developing order of actions so lucidly symbolic of a developing state of spirit—from moment to moment, so morally identifiable—as to suggest the conditions of allegory without forfeiting or even subordinating the realistic "superficial" claim of the actions and their actors. . . .

The problem is, of course, Kurtz. It is when we are on the verge of meeting Kurtz that Marlow's "inconceivables" and "impenetrables" begin to multiply at an alarming rate; it is when we have already met him that we are urged to observe "smiles of indefinable meaning" and to hear about "unspeakable rites" and "gratified and monstrous passions" and "subtle horrors"—words to hound the reader into a sense of enigmatic awfulness that he would somehow be the better for not trying to find a way through. . . . Unhappily, though, the effect . . . is to bring to mind and penetrate Conrad's magazine-writer style as well as the hollowness of Kurtz's sentiments.

—Marvin Mudrick, "The Originality of Conrad," 1959

On Comparing the Two Works

"The Secret Sharer" is forthright in structure and simple in style, as direct and immediate and frightening as any very personal diary. *Heart of Darkness*, on the other hand, is evasive in structure and even uncomfortably wordy. Words! At times Conrad and Marlow seem to want to erect (as does a psychoanalyst's patient) a screen of words between themselves and the horror of a half-remembered experience.

. . . But both stories are also dramas of consciousness and conscience, symbolic explorations of inward complexity. They are . . . stories of youth's initiation into manhood and knowledge, dramatized testings of personal strength and integrity, psychological studies in half-conscious *identification*. Why does Marlow seek out and remain loyal to the unspeakable and savage Kurtz in *Heart of Darkness*? Why does the narrator (the "I") of "The Secret Sharer" protect the criminally impulsive Leggatt? Both have identified themselves, temporarily, with these outcast and more primitive beings; lived vicariously in them. In the unconscious mind of each of us slumber infinite capacities for reversion and crime. And our best chance for survival, moral survival, lies in frankly recognizing these capacities.

—Albert J. Guerard, "Introduction"
to the Signet Classic edition, 1950

On "The Secret Sharer": A Skeptical View

Usually, in the face of a work improperly understood, critics blame one another; but in this case the work itself is at fault. Although "The Secret Sharer" is a fascinating and provocative story, its details are at times so vaguely portentous that readers are seduced into hunting for a complex symbolic consistency which the work does not possess. . . . Because of its insistent promptings and seductive detail, "The Secret Sharer" has become everybody's Rorschach test.

—Lawrence Graver, *Conrad's Short
Fiction*, 1969